From Plowing

by

Lester Swope

****

****

Dedication

I dedicate this book to my grandparents Carl and Fannie Park they have influenced me my entire life to obey and follow Jesus. They taught me that *if I am trusting Jesus to take me to heaven when I die, then I should obey His teaching while I am living.*

Jesus said, *"teaching them to obey everything I have commanded you..."* (Matthew 18:20 NIV).

****

Jesus came and told his disciples, "I have been given all authority in heaven and on earth. Therefore, go and make disciples of all the nations, baptizing them in the name of the Father and the Son and the Holy Spirit. Teach these new disciples to obey all the commands I have given you. And be sure of this: I am with you always, even to the end of the age." (Matthew 28:18-20 NLT)

****

Contents

****

Part I
The Call

But ***even if you suffer for doing what is right, God will reward you for it****. So don't worry or be afraid of their threats. Instead, you must worship Christ as Lord of your life. And* ***if someone asks about your hope as a believer, always be ready to explain it****.*
(1 Peter 3:14-15 NLT)

****

Introduction

> *It is different here than we probably even realized and we truly need God's help. And so do the Haitians. They are nicer people than I even realized people could be; very kind and friendly, yet good humored for their hard way of life...*
>
> *We hope and pray that something we say here will be of help to the people. Most of all spiritually. We tend to forget that while we live in nice houses, half of the world sleeps under a grass roof.* –Borel, Haiti, November 4, 1967

I was born late in 1939, and born again early in 1955. I lived an unusual, atypical life ranging from farming in rural Pennsylvania to preaching Christ on the island of Haiti.

The son of Lorainne and Elloise Swope, I was the first of three children, followed by sister, Bonnie; and brother, Dwight. Following the Great Depression, in 1941, my parents had moved from rural Pennsylvania to Wilkinsburg, a suburb of Pittsburgh. The years following the Depression, and going into World War II, were serious and uncertain. This was the America I was born into.

We lived in an apartment for a couple of years and then dad bought a three story house and remodeled it so there was room for three different apartments. We lived in one and rented out the other two for income. Dad worked for the defense industry during World War II, running metal presses to build airplane propellor hubs and airbrakes for trains. Dad was the fifth child of ten—the fifth son in a row, followed by twin sisters, then another brother, and two more sisters. Of course he thought the girls received all the attention.

***

When I was 7 years old, with my parents' consent, I left my childhood home in Pittsburgh and moved to Maddensville to be with my grandparents. Most of my youth was lived in rural Pennsylvania, between Big Aughwick Creek and Black Log Mountain, in Huntingdon County. My "hometown" was quite literally a *town* at my *home*. Maddensville was a very small village located in the middle of my grandfather's farm. The store, post office, and the shops were all there.

Even at the age of 7, I knew I belonged on a farm. I wanted out of the city and out of that house. In the mid-1940s, my grandfather on my mother's side, Carl Park, was in the process of securing a farm I simply had to be there.

Except for a couple of years during the war, Grandpap was a farmer, except when he worked at his brother-in-law's ice plant in Harrisburg for a couple of years before moving back to Huntingdon County in 1946.

I pushed the idea to go live on my grandparents farm every chance I got. And I still have the letter I wrote in 1946 to my grandmother, Fannie Park, that says:

Dear Grandma,
I am still waiting for you to get the farm.
Did Granpap change his mind about the farm?
I am ready to go farming.

That following Christmas, it was a done deal.

I was in second grade and during Christmas break I packed up my duds; and when we went to see the grandparents, I took my stuff along and stayed. While there wasn't much farming to do in the middle of winter, I loved being with my grandparents. The holiday season only accentuated the warmth of the moment all the more so.

***

A quick peek back beyond my grandparents.

My dad's side of the family originated from Germany, and my mother's family from England. An ancestor by the name of Richard Lane arrived with his wife and five children from England to Providence Island in 1635. Richard, who at one time was nominated to be governor of the island, would later drown off the coast of the island alongside his youngest son, Oziell.

The oldest son, Samuel, eventually moved to the mainland and settled in Maryland in 1663 with a party of immigrants. In 1669, Samuel inherited 300 acres of land known as Bromley Hall from Richard Wells, who died in 1671 and left his entire estate to Samuel.

The Lane family settled throughout the southeastern and mid-Atlantic portions of what was to become the United States of America.

***

While I was living an idyllic life on the farm with my grandparents, meanwhile, 1,576 miles south of Pennsylvania, the Caribbean island of Haiti had just experienced yet another of many revolutions. In 1946, the citizens elected a former school teacher as president. Operating under a new constitution that went into effect in November of that year, Haitian president Léon Dumarsais Estimé began to bring about long-overdue changes in the nation's economy and education systems.

But like so many leaders in Haiti's long and tumultuous history, Estimé would be overthrown in 1950. He succumbed to the pitfalls of personal ambition and the creature comforts of holding office, as did many before and after him. Unfortunately, it would be very a long time before the nation of Haiti would see a presidential candidate who displayed a genuine concern for the welfare of the people.

Little did I know God would call me to share the Gospel with the people of this small, troubled island in the middle of the Caribbean Sea.

****

1
Roots

And they overcame him by the blood of the Lamb, and by the word of their testimony; and they loved not their lives unto the death (Revelation 12:11).

I spent nearly my entire youth living on three farms where lush rolling hills and good rich earth captured my attention and imagination daily. First, I worked on Grandfather Carl's farm, then my parents', and then a farm of my own.

I had a different hope but same desire to farm, illustrating the dichotomy I confess I often struggled with in my youth. I was saved by Christ but not committed to Christ. The more I got, the less peace I had. The more I went to church, the more troubled I became. Christ didn't control my life. The cows did. I was geared to making money. Reading to put in time.

At first, I had the promise that I would go to Heaven when I died; and my sins were forgiven. For ten years, I struggled with the problem of going to church and reading the Bible—but not putting it into practice. I was told by the church just to sit back and relax, go to church, that's all there is to the Christian life. But verses like Matthew 7:24 burned in my mind. Jesus said, *"Therefore everyone who hears these words of mine and puts them into practice is like a wise man who built his house on the rock."*

In my teens, I began reading nonfiction books including *Through the Gates of Splendor* by Elisabeth Elliot, and stories of missionaries such as Hudson Taylor, C.T. Stud, John and Betty Stam, Paul Carlson, and others. I was left with more unanswered questions regarding my relationship with Christ, but was fascinated by the testimonies of these brave men and women of God.

One night I was unable to sleep, so I read *God Planted Five Seeds* by Jean Dye Johnson—and then I *really* couldn't sleep! Reading the story of five men who traveled deep into the Bolivian jungle to bring the gospel to the Ayore people shook me to my core. How these brave men's martyrdom blazed the trail for future missionaries to win the Ayores to Christ both inspired and terrified me.

I was reading all the books about missionaries that I could get my hands on, and in 1955, at age 15, with a little persuasion from my grandfather, I decided that farming and reading books meant nothing without Jesus. During one of my home church's revival services, when the preacher gave the altar call invitation, I stood to my feet in front of the entire assembly and publicly devoted my life to the service of God.

Train up a child in the way he should go, and when he is old he will not depart from it (Proverbs 22:6 NIV).

***

I was happily busy during the years on my grandparents' farm, enjoying the company of Granpap, working with him from dawn until dusk. While we were in the fields together, he was always very affirmative and encouraging. I loved him and the work. Life was good.

Outside of school and farming I have few memories of that time other than occasionally fishing at a nearby creek with a friend from church.

Decades later, I wrote in my journal:

> *There was nothing in this world that I would rather do than work with my Grandpap. It was never a chore or burden working with him. There was always a source of encouragement from him. When the day was done, he would always compliment and encourage me for the amount of work that we had accomplished.*
> *Grandpap Carl told me about delivering farm machinery and setting it up, hauling coal with a team from the mine at Joller, grading the road and pulling a dump wagon with a team when the road to Maddensville was built, while farming at the same time....*
> *Most of everything that has happened to me was due to the influence of my Grandparents, including the calling to be a missionary, pastor, and evangelist and planting churches.*

My grandmother was a significant influence in her own right, she exemplified what a Christian grandmother should be. I wrote of her:

Grandma's influence has spanned a century. She was 50 when she started raising me and she didn't seem old to me at that time. She planted a huge garden, canned, butchered, heated water in an iron kettle over a wood fire to wash clothes and made lye soap out of leftover fat. I remember her cooking on a wood stove and the time when she bought her first refrigerator. Before that, she kept things cold in water at the pump house. She never wasted anything; our clothes were patched until they ended up as braided rugs on the floor.
It was Grandma who taught me to visit the sick. She would take me along with her to visit people who were dying at home.... She would visit people no matter who they were.
She taught me great respect for the things of God and encouraged me every step of the way in becoming a missionary and a pastor.

My uncle, Wayne Park, a younger brother of my mom, helped at the farm. A WWII veteran, Uncle Wayne was a quiet man who had served in the U.S. Navy on landing ships. He told stories like the time when he was in the South Pacific Ocean taking supplies to shore in the Pacific Islands. The ship's diesel engine failed enroute, and the vessel and crew had to return to base, while another ship took their place in the fleet. That ship struck a Japanese mine that exploded, killing and wounding several men.

Uncle Wayne also told of how he could stand on the deck of his ship at night and watch tracer bullets from the Japanese raining down like shooting stars from the mountains. They were too far away to hit the ships, so he would stand and watch the bullets flashing across the night sky as if a fireworks show.

I wasn't close with Uncle Wayne or Aunt Irene. Not like I was with my grandfather. But farming alongside family was still great joy. And there was certainly enough farmland on both sides of the family to go around.

Dad's parents, Millard and Josie Swope, also lived in Huntingdon County. Grandad Millard passed away when I was less than a year old, and Grandmom Josie passed away when I was 21. I visited her from time to time on their farm—she was a great cook.

***

My great-grandparents, Dutton and Elizabeth Lane, owned a general store in Meadowgap, Pennsylvania. Then they moved to the small village of Pogue and built a store and gas station, not far from where my mother grew up in Three Springs. Dutton passed away, and when Elizabeth passed in 1950, one of my great-aunts purchased the property. When a nearby farm went up for sale, my dad promptly bought it.

By this time, I had been working with my grandfather for several years, and had some cattle of my own. After my parents bought the farm, they persuaded me to bring my cattle and live with them.

That was a mistake. I had a very good relationship with my grandfather and farming with him was great. Unfortunately, it wasn't too long after I was back with my parents that conflict started.
Working with Dad was much different from working with Granpap. I tried to do what was right and do my part. And I think my father knew that, but Dad's critical eye was a stark contrast to the affirmation given by Granpap.

To compound matters, Mom had decided she wanted nothing to do with the farm. Therefore, she never spoke up or got involved concerning any grievances around the farm, thus making herself unavailable when I wanted to confide in her.

I did confide in Granpap about Dad's attitude. But this only created some tension between the two. My grandfather was not a confrontational person. But he did lend support, and knew how critical Dad could be. He knew I always worked as hard as I could and did as much as I could.

Although I loved farm work, the older I got the more I thought about a social life or playing sports. But there was no discussion about it with my parents—farm work was the top and only priority.

***

On the weekends, my sister, Bonnie, would travel from Harrisburg to help on the farm. We were very close and had fun working together. During the week she worked in the State Capitol.

Then she moved back to Huntingdon County where she met her future husband, David Reed.
David worked in the printing business and Bonnie had an insurance job, both in Huntingdon. Soon, both Bonnie and David were spending weekends on the farms, visiting and helping with the chores. They married and had a daughter, my niece, Jill.

Sundays were the only days off from farming, so we could as a family attend church.

Between church activities and the farm, I was way too preoccupied to get into the kinds of trouble most youth get into. A friend from church and I would occasionally go fishing at a stream near my grandparents' farm. Apart from that, church and farming with family was my way of life throughout most of my childhood and into my mid-twenties.

I was brought up in church and pretty much churched before moving back in with my parents. My grandparents had an enormous influence on my faith, taking me to many revival services throughout Huntingdon County. Attending those evangelistic services and hearing those preachers actually taught me how to preach.

***

In my early twenties, I began a courtship with Dolores Horne, the sister of my fishing friend, Fred. She was a year younger and we attended the same church, Walnut Grove Church of God.

We had grown up together. I knew her from church and from singing in the church choir. The choir sang at other churches during revival; and because I had a car then, I would ask her if she needed lift to the church where we were going to sing. That's when we started going together—I was almost 20.

We married in 1960, and the next year our first son, Jeff, was born. Then at the age of 24, while still working on my parent's farm, I purchased a farm that came to be known as "The Giles Farm." The year was 1964, and the American Dream was beginning to take shape for me and my family.

The farm had 150 acres—100 acres of creek bottom—really good land for farming. I bought it in 1964, just in time to plant the crops that spring. Like many young people, I thought I had life all figured out. The more land I owned, the more crops I could raise; the more cows I could milk, the more milk I could sell; and the more money I would make.

***

But this perception of life's meaning was eventually shattered, not only by the diet of literature I so often consumed, but by a sudden realization of life's fleetingness. In 1966, my beloved Granpap Carl passed away. As difficult as that was, my only sister, Bonnie, passed away that same year. She passed on a Friday evening and I was planning to visit her Saturday morning.

Bonnie died of Leukemia at the age of 23. I was 26. Our younger brother, Dwight, was only12.

In the beginning of January 1966 she tired very quickly and was exhausted. The doctors determined she had leukemia and sent her to the University of Pennsylvania Hospital in Philadelphia. She was treated with experimental medications, with no certainty of how they would affect her. For the next three months, I watched as she suffered. Making matters worse, Bonnie had been pregnant at the time she fell ill, and her daughter Jill was only one and a half years old. She eventually lost the baby due to the infection, before succumbing to the cancer herself.

On the first day of April in the year 1966, Bonnie Swope Reed went home to be with the Lord.

We drove to Philadelphia that Friday evening and were asked if we wanted to go in to see her. When we saw that she passed with a smile on her face—it was most remarkable and memorable and brought a sense of comfort to see my sister smiling one last time.

That was the way she lived—with a smile on her face for everyone. She was very active in the church, very committed to Christ, and very friendly and social. Although I had a sense of peace, my parents didn't handle Bonnie's death very well. In fact, they didn't handle it at all.

Period. They really never got over it. Dwight, being the youngest, was influenced by our parents' terrible grief.

***

After her passing, Bonnie's body could not be immediately transported back to Huntingdon County from Philadelphia because an autopsy had to be completed. So, our pastor could sense that I was struggling emotionally and invited me to a Sunday evening church service in place of the service that had been planned for Bonnie's viewing. It was postponed because of the autopsy. The service that evening was a missions presentation by a visiting missionary from Haiti.

I knew I was being called to the missions field, but the idea had always been somewhat frightening. With both my grandfather and sister gone, I had much less reluctance and decided to go hear what the missionary had to say. I realized that if I was going to do anything regarding the call on my life, I needed to do it right then—because the future is very uncertain.

This one decision set the course for the rest of my life.

****

2
Learning to Pivot

"For I know the plans I have for you," says the Lord. "They are plans for good and not for disaster, to give you a future and a hope" (Jeremiah 29:11 NLT).

On April 1, 1966, a missionary from Haiti spoke at Cherry Grove Church of God in Huntingdon County. I was in attendance that evening. Having already filled my head with countless books about mission trips and missionary testimonies, I knew that a pivotal moment had arrived.

God called me and I knew I was destined for Haiti. Neither cows nor farm could change that. Though I knew God was calling me to a higher purpose, I didn't yet see that He was calling me to a spiritual destination as well—to a place where I would have to wrestle with spiritual enemies I never imagined while a youth in Pennsylvania.

In time, I learned the truth within the words of Ephesians 6:12 (NIV): *"For our struggle is not against flesh and blood, but against the rulers, against the authorities, against the powers of this dark world and against the spiritual forces of evil in the heavenly realms."*

I felt called. So I talked to our pastor and he said the church was opening a mission in Haiti and needed people to fill positions there and there were some for which I was qualified.
Hearing the missionary from Haiti speak that night confirmed God's calling for me.

***

The preacher was extremely persuasive. According to some, the bombastic missionary could coerce just about anybody to give him a vehicle or even jewelry. After serving in the military during the war, he had served some years with another church organization in Haiti before he persuaded the denomination at my church into supporting him. He was soon appointed to be the missions director, or as the Haitians would say, *"gro chef."*

The very Sunday evening that my family and I had planned to attend a viewing for Bonnie, I instead was listening to a fiery message about the incredible need for help in the Caribbean island-nation of Haiti. At least *this* much of what the missionary said was true.

I was naïve and didn't realize that a lot of what he was telling people the church was far from the truth. He persuaded women to take their wedding rings off and put them in the offering plate. He had a tremendous ability to influence people.

In spite of all that, it was as clear to me that the Lord had opened a doorway to a new life and new assignment for me and my family. By the time 1967 arrived, Dolores and I had already made preparations to sell our property and move to Haiti. We had spent the entire seven years of our married life, and all of our son Jeff's life on The Farm. Now we were facing a future of uncertainty. The only certainty we had—and the only certainty we truly needed—was knowing that God would take care of us in spite of any circumstance.

During the months of preparation, I had contacted the missionary with questions and concerns. I wanted more details about the mission and what we could expect when we arrived in Haiti. I was also hoping to develop rapport with the man who was to become my leader in Haiti. Letter after letter went unanswered, with one final exception.

When I asked him if he needed anything, he sent me a long list of what he needed; a deep well submersible pump, a rototiller, and other expensive items. So of course I bought it all and took it along when we went. But he never did answer any of my questions or gave me any idea of what to expect.

Looking back, my lack of honest communication should have been the first red flag. I had a pretty idealistic view of the church, and of preachers and missionaries, so I never thought to second guess his credibility or motives.

***

In the meantime, I contacted an auctioneer about selling my cows and farming machinery. The auctioneer said it was too late in the spring for an auction because farmers had already started planting. Getting them to come to a sale would be difficult as they would be too busy in their fields to attend an auction.

Not only was it the farm machinery but the entire farm itself had to go. And to compound matters, there was only one auction date available, April 29, which was only three weeks away. This was not nearly enough time to do the all the proper advertising; at least not in the pre-Internet and pre-cell phone days of 1967. I had to get the word out the old-fashioned way.

Nevertheless, I told the auctioneer that I'd take the date. The rest I left up to God. And as He would so many times, God came through.

One day a young artist strolled into Huntingdon County and mentioned to a clerk at a nearby country store that he was in the area looking for a piece of property to purchase that was "way back in the hills."

My farm was across a large creek. To get there people had to travel through the hills more than a mile down a lane.

The young man was interested in peace and privacy, so the salesman sent him to see me. We negotiated, but couldn't agree on a price. A few days later, I called and said I would take his offer. He said he was sorry but he had just bought property and spent his money.

I wasn't disappointed because I was trusting God. I knew God had called me to Haiti. I didn't know what to do with the farm but I don't believe you can have any regrets wondering if something was God's will. But also, I don't believe that you should be stupid about important decisions. I had a calm assurance I was doing the right thing.

However, the situation posed a challenge because I still owed the bank for the cows, farm machinery, and the farm itself. The banker said I owed too much money and he wouldn't allow me to have the sale.

My father took it upon himself to speak to the banker, and told the banker he would sign the note for the amount owed to the bank. Then made an agreement with the banker—allowing me to have the sale, so long as I would allow him to come and collect the money on the day of the sale, in person.

I called the auctioneer and told him to add the farm to the sale bill! Then I called the young artist and told him that the farm would be up for auction on April 29. This I did, in spite of knowing that the man had already purchased property.

As it turned out, the young artist had bought property in New York. Therefore, he was still looking for suitable property in rural Pennsylvania.

He bid it up to the price that I had set, so I told the auctioneer to knock it off to him. The farm brought almost twice the amount that I had paid three years prior.

When the sale was over, Dad asked the banker how much he received. He said $46,000. The total of all of my debts was $23,000. Dad asked the banker, "Are you satisfied, sir?" The banker told me to come to the bank on Monday to settle up. Then he asked me where I wanted to put the money. I told him to put it all in a checking account, and give me one blank check.

God blessed me immeasurably—more than I asked or imagined. God led me all the way.

> *Now to Him who is able to do exceedingly abundantly above all that we ask or think, according to the power that works in us to Him be glory in the church by Christ Jesus to all generations, forever and ever. Amen* (Ephesians 3:20-21 NKJV).

Through it all, my dear wife, Dolores, remained supportive. She had always known of my desire to do missions work, and that I had heard the call of God on our lives.

In the midst of all the planning, my brother-in-law, Fred Horne, approached me about Haiti. When Fred came to talk to me I thought he was going to offer to take care of the farm if it wasn't sold at the public sale. But instead, he and Nancy were interested in applying to go to Haiti.

I was surprised, as Dolores's brother had not been married long when they decided to follow God's call too. They also wanted to go because Dolores and I were going, and they wanted to accompany us. The Horns lived in Haiti for twenty years, having three children while there.

My future was a bit less clear-cut, as I would eventually begin to realize.

Right before we went to Haiti, an evangelist taught us the words to this song:

I'll live for Jesus day after day,
I'll live for Jesus, let come what may;
The Holy Spirit I will obey,
And live for Jesus, day after day.

Many, many times over the coming years when I was working on a project or feeling melancholy, I'd realize that I was singing that song to myself. A calm would come over me knowing that Jesus was with me day by day by day. I knew God called me to Haiti and His voice was leading me each step of the way through the sale of the farm and property, in spite of all obstacles.

During the time of preparation, the Churches of God, General Conference (CGGC) had not yet responded to my application request to travel to Haiti. But I didn't need to hear from them—I had heard from God.

Not until the very eve of the auction did the CGGC's Commission of World Missions contact me to inform me what I already knew deep down in my spirit—the Swopes were on our way to Haiti.

> *Behold, I send you out as sheep in the midst of wolves. Therefore be wise as serpents and harmless as doves* (Matthew 10:16 NKJV).

***

It may be reasonable to say that I knew next to nothing about Haiti before setting foot there. A friend of mine at church gave me a *National Geographic* magazine. I think I still have it. So that was about the extent of what I knew.

The CGGC informed us that we needed to be in Haiti by June that summer.

On June 20, 1967, our pastor along with his wife, Dolores' parents, and my mom were all at the airport to see us off, to bid us a fond farewell. Dolores, six-year-old son Jeff, and I, would stop over in Florida where we would board a connecting flight to Port-au-Prince, Haiti.

We departed the airport in Harrisburg, Pennsylvania, at 10:17 a.m. A young family from the middle of rural Pennsylvania had just turned our backs on every earthly thing we had ever known to travel to a distant nation with a very fascinating and sad story to tell.

It was not long after the engines fired up and the propellers began to swirl that my tears began to run like the Aughwick Creek that ran through the farm where we used to live.

***

Missionary work was challenging. I began writing in a journal, which was both comforting and cathartic. Although my entries were sporadic at times, writing became my way of expressing myself when it would've been improper to do so otherwise. Being a relatively timid and sheltered young man, nothing could have prepared me for what my family and I would encounter in Haiti. Not the least of which were the wolves in sheep clothing.

My most intimidating adversary was the very man who partly inspired me to go to Haiti in the first place. Not long after we arrived in Haiti, I learned that gro chef's talk and his walk were not the same.

****

3
Off We Go

We boarded our plane for Haiti. We got to fly first class. They served champagne about every hour, and the stewardess said we were a funny family because we refused the drinks. We left Port-au-Prince at 9 pm and didn't get to Borel until 3 am. What a ride. I'll never forget.

Dolores Swope's Diary Entry
June 21, 1967 ~ 4:30 p.m.

Night time fell over the Caribbean islands as our plane approached François Duvalier International Airport in Port-au-Prince. The capitol city is one of Haiti's largest centers of economy and finance. Though some assert Port-au-Prince's reputation as a dangerous city, it has been an important center for global commerce for more than two centuries, due much to Haiti's exports of sugar, coffee, cocoa, textiles, cement, essential oils, seafood, and tropical fruit.

Because we arrived at the airport after dark, we walked down a dimly lit flight of stairs and across the airport tarmac to a small metal building. The interior was lit with only a few light bulbs dangling on the end of long wires from the rafters overhead. The room was filled with shadowy figures. Many of the men carried M1 carbine rifles, a standard U.S. military firearm at that time.

As we neared the men, I realized that my family and I had never encountered black people face-to-face before. Young Jeff was curiously mesmerized and calm even while being frisked, along with Dolores and I. Frisks and searches were common for travelers in Haiti. It was an experience that would soon become routine for us at every roadblock. Jeff never complained or fussed about it and there were many road-blocks between Port-au-Prince and Borel, our destination.

After what was essentially a routine security procedure, we and other passengers were allowed into the country. Waiting at the airport was the Director of Missions for Project Help, Haiti. Also waiting was gro chef who arrived with a small pickup truck that was already quite full of members of his own family. Gro chef, a tall, large man, chose to sit on the roof of the truck. There was just enough room next to him for me to sit, while everyone else climbed into the truck bed.

At that point we were not yet aware that our arrival in Haiti came at a time when the national turmoil had reached a critical point. We received very little information about Haiti from the Commission of World Missions and even less from gro chef. We knew very little about the country of Haiti and even less about where we would live.

Some of what gro chef told me that first night up on the truck roof with him gave me a sinking feeling that things were not what they seemed to be. At one point, in a rather surprising and arrogant manner, gro chef leaned over and made it very clear that he, and only he, was in charge. He told me, "The Church of God has no right and no claim to the mission, or the land or the buildings, or whatever"—because *he* was in control. Right then I should have knocked on the roof to get the driver's attention to stop and let us off the truck and departed. If I had any sense, I should have read between the lines. But all I knew for sure was that God called me there.

After a hot and bumpy 80-mile journey north of the capitol, we arrived at the village of Borel, and the campus for Project Help. Just outside the gate of the compound was a government security office with armed guards. Just inside the compound was a school building that would double as a church until a proper place of worship could be constructed. Beyond that was a dormitory building, and not much else. The electrical wiring had been stripped out of the buildings. They were just shells.

I quickly learned there was no house for us to live in—as we were led to believe. A small, abandoned house miles from the campus was our only option.

***

Borel is a settlement in the Artibonite Valley; a relatively self-sufficient community with most of the population consuming goods produced from nearby family farms in a rural neighborhood. It's about 80 miles inland, north of Port-au-Prince. The Artibonite River flows through the valley, with some of its waters flowing from the Dominican Republic. The entire region is largely rural with no public electricity.

Back in 1967, there were some small markets to buy locally grown produce. But for most other items, we went to Port-au-Prince.

I was profoundly affected by the poverty surrounding us. Most people lived in small wood houses with grass roofs. The primary modes of transportation were by horse, mule, or on foot. Few outside the elite class or the government could afford automobiles. I began to realize that not many people have a very nice in life. They don't have what we have in the United States—food, housing, even the necessities of life.

Now aware that I'd spent life in a relative bubble, I became more determined to press on.

The plans to grow Project Help in Borel weren't complex, but would require a lot of hard work. The compound already had buildings for school. Over time it would grow to house churches, elementary and vocational schools. However, there were no living quarters for the time being.

The families learned they would be staying in some buildings not far from Borel, in Deschapelles, another community between the two mountain ranges that make up the Artibonite Valley. Deschapelles sits about five miles west of the nearest city, Verettes.

Our family's house was a small cement block structure with a tin roof and louvered windows. It was one of a series of buildings at that location, that once belonged to the U.S. Standard Fruit Company in the 1930s and '40s, when the company used to pay local growers in Haiti to produce bananas.

The houses were small but adequate. Gro chef said he had possession of two of these buildings. In one of them we all shared a kitchen, and the other was used for bedrooms. He had us move into one of the two buildings, and the kitchen was in the house where he lived.

Standing out among the small community of Deschapelles was the Albert Schweitzer Hospital of Haiti, built in 1956 by an American philanthropist and his wife. To this day, the hospital has been the primary source of healthcare for the surrounding region, as well as the largest employer in the area; although most people in the valley work as subsistence farmers.

The Deschapelles area of the valley is productive for rice growing. There are also many small businesses such as carpenters, tailors, craftsmen, and a market area.

Soon enough, the Swope and Horne families met the local Haitian pastors with whom we would be spending the foreseeable future at Project Help as well as several lay people and many older teenage boys who were often hired to help with various projects.

Nearly everyone who worked for Project Help spoke some English, and I soon began learning Creole, the preferred language among most Haitians.

I became fast friends with Pastor Jules Bolier, a Haitian reverend about 15 years older than I was. He was rather large for a Haitian, a tall and hefty man and very kind, not intimidating. I trusted him from the beginning and supported his work financially.

Pastor Jules had a church of his own nearby, and he worked for Project Help. He was also building an orphanage, and I happily lent a hand. Thus began a lifelong friendship. By God's grace, much of the most important information, advice, and assistance that I and my family received while in Haiti came from Pastor Jules. He was not only a reverend, teacher, and church planter, he also worked for Albert Schweitzer Hospital. And he taught Creole and became my Creole teacher.

Pastors Jerome and Joseph were both from Cap-Haitien, a large city on the northern coast. Both were in their early to mid-20s and had a desire and a vision to spread the Gospel, with a willingness to go into new areas and plant churches. They wanted to be used of God. Both of them were of that mindset and were consistently committed. I could count on them and often worked alongside these two men. Joseph was in the beginning stages of starting a church in Saint Marc and I occasionally attended his church with my new friends.

Reverend Domeleon was the eldest of the local clergy hired for Project Help. He preferred to be called Brother Domeleon, or "frè Do," for short. The Creole word "frè" meaning "brother." His humble nature kept him from feeling the elevated need to be called reverend or pastor. Although Brother Domelion worked for Project Help, he also shepherded a number of local church communities that, like Pastor Jules, he had planted.

Although frè Do was frail, asthmatic, and nearly 60 years of age, he was a passionate church planter. He was small of stature but he had a big, big heart. He went all over the island on his own—to the mountains to the end of the valley at the ocean. Wherever he could go to plant a church, he went; and he was pretty successful.

We saw frè Do regularly. In the evenings, it was his routine to hold prayer meetings in the villages. If the attendance was good and there was enough interest, frè Do would plant a church. I often attended these meetings. He often wore a pair of pullover gumboots that came up to his knees. He got them from working on the canal and became his regular work boots. He was a local pastor at a little church before Project Help, and then gro chef persuaded him to work for us.

Frè Do was paid a much lower wage than the other staff and pastors received. But, as far as I know, frè Do never made an issue of it, even though none of the other pastors did as much church planting and evangelizing as he did. He was very humble and didn't ask for things, or cry the blues.

As Project Help grew, gro chef convinced frè Do to turn over his ministry to come under the banner of Project Help—frè Do was happy to oblige. Gro chef later laid claim to the churches frè Do had begun, crediting them to himself and his work for Project Help. It wasn't illegal, but it surely wasn't ethical to take the credit for another person's hard work. But frè Do cared more about saving souls than who got the credit, or how much money he made.

This was one of several unethical practices of gro chef that I couldn't help noticing. But I purposed to keep my thoughts and opinions to myself—for the time being.

There was Pastor Lulu, who seemed friendly enough on the outside, but like the gro chef, had another agenda.

Pastor Chaplet took the middle of the road approach to most everything. He seemed to know what was going on in the country and was aware of what was happening with gro chef. He had a few connections in the government, so often times he would share news with us. Other than that, he just collected his salary and didn't get involved.

And then there was Felix Latonda who often rode a bicycle and appeared to be a plain-clothed officer or government official of some kind. I never did get around to asking Felix the truth of it. In all the time I had interactions with the man, never once did he mention what his job was, although he occasionally let hints slip through.

Felix never dressed in a uniform or seemed to carry a weapon; but it became clearer over time that he had connections within the Haitian government, as well as some means and privileges most Haitian citizens did not have. Typically, the most lucrative means of employment in Haiti are government jobs. If Felix was a local officer of some kind, it would seem he was only interested in keeping the peace and collecting a paycheck. This was the case with many of the soldiers based at Borel. Thankfully, Fred's family and my family got along just fine with them. Felix and I hit it off right away. Felix regularly volunteered his time to act as a Creole interpreter on my behalf, and accompanied me on errands. He was very friendly and I took a liking to him. He was probably about my age and very impressive.

Adding more variety to the cast of characters in our new life, we learned that our "house," which sat next door to the Albert Schweitzer Hospital, was directly adjacent to the home of none other than William Larimer Mellon Jr., a renowned American philanthropist and physician, and also a Pennsylvania native. He and his wife, Gwen, built the Albert Schweitzer Hospital of Haiti, in Deschapelles, and they lived on the grounds next to the old Standard Fruit buildings where we called home.

His father, William Sr., was a wealthy financier who had built a family fortune derived from Gulf Oil, Westinghouse, and Alcoa corporations, to name a few. William Jr., "Larry" and his wife moved to Haiti in 1956 when they opened the hospital, and remained there ever since.

We were neighbors with the Mellons for only a brief time while we were between houses, but I remember seeing them often, especially when we were at the hospital. Unfortunately, visits to the hospital became a regularity for our whole family. Our Pennsylvanian immune systems were not ready to handle the variety of illnesses common in tropical breeding grounds of bacteria and disease.

Nevertheless, we managed to grow very comfortable, spending our days with the Haitians, and soon began making friends. Much is often said about the Haitian peoples' resiliency and their propensity for laughter in the face of harsh circumstances—and our rural American family was experiencing first-hand the Haitians' welcoming kindness and joy. It took no time at all for Haiti to find its way into our hearts. I was only in Haiti a short time before I realized that agriculture was not their total need, the Gospel was.

This obvious need of my newfound neighbors prompted me to be bolder than ever before—than I even thought possible. However, it would nearly get me in trouble more than once.

***

One day, later that year, a black, bulletproof Mercedes 600 limousine pulled into Borel; along with a number of trucks carrying armed men. Out of the limousine stepped a somewhat frail man in his late 50s, wearing a top hat and thick glasses and with an odd smirk that seemed almost permanently etched on his face. He was Haiti's infamous and despotic president, François Duvalier.

Gro chef cordially welcomed him, which was no surprise to me. I had noticed that gro chef was often obsequious, or schmoozy, with anyone who seemed powerful and influential, including the soldiers stationed at the campus.

I knew next to nothing about Haiti's self-appointed "President for Life," but had seen enough of Haiti already to know that this guy was not a good leader. I found it absurd that a president would be out on the "campaign trail" when there was no one running against him.

When Duvalier announced to everyone who gathered around that he was out doing some campaigning for president, I had the audacity to jokingly blurt out, "Who's the other candidate?" to some teens standing next to me. My Haitian cohorts quickly urged me to be silent, perhaps fearing for their lives. They understood that the "campaign" was likely propaganda to keep the international community appeased.

This type of political theater was common for Duvalier, who would sometimes have himself filmed while touring Port-au-Prince, as crowds of excited people ran after his limousine. In the footage they appear to love their president, when in reality, he was handing petty cash out the car window.

No one dared question or challenge François Duvalier's actions without incurring his wrath. However, it seemed neither Duvalier, nor his militia, heard my sarcastic question that day. Or perhaps by a miracle, they chose to ignore it.

I was more brass than brains back then. Maybe I thought I could change things. I soon learned that I didn't have any say in the politics. I was interested, but I had no way or reason to be involved.

****

4
Decades of Death—Generations of Life

If you see the poor oppressed in a district, and justice and rights denied, do not be surprised at such things; for one official is eyed by a higher one, and over them both are others higher still (Ecclesiastes 5:8 NIV).

Our arrival in Haiti was during the most infamous times in the nation's history. Ten years earlier, Haiti underwent severe political turmoil—an all too common occurrence that has plagued the nation since its infancy, and continues today as Haiti's President Jovenel Moise was assassinated in his home in 2021. He was a former banana exporter and divisive figure in Haitian politics who throughout his presidency had failed to hold elections at local and national levels. Such was the same now as it was then in 1967 when we arrived.

The day after we landed in Haiti and after the grueling trip in the truck, we were quite tired and Dolores was terribly sick. Jeff and I went with the men to work at Borel. It was a long day. It rained in the afternoon, so we got a good night's sleep when it cooled down.

The daily hard work in extreme heat at Borel proved to be quite discouraging. My first assignment was to clear an area around the perimeter of the compound in order to put up a fence. I was to cut down several dozen mature mango trees—an important food source. The thought of going through with this task in a starving nation troubled me greatly. For years I had imagined being involved in missions work; and yet on his first day, *this* is the assignment I was given. I felt I had no option but to follow orders.

It was very disturbing to me—I would be cutting down enough mango trees to feed a hundred to a thousand people. I was to cut them down and make firewood. Gro chef didn't want any trees around the fence; there were a lot of things on my mind regarding gro chef.

As if being ordered to chop down fruit trees in a poor country wasn't unsettling enough, just as disturbing were his next instructions, and the reasons for them.

He told me that we had to put up a chain link fence and not to use the rather soft wire—I was to use steel wire that was impossible to cut. He said, "I want you to cut these wires all new. I don't want that softer wire because *they* could cut through it." By "they," he meant the Haitians. It was obvious at this point that the reasons for putting up a fence weren't simply to mark the property line or keep animals out, it was also for security.

It seemed to me that gro chef had an almost paranoid attitude toward the local people. He often made it clear that he didn't want any Haitians wandering around on the property. But if his attitude toward the Haitians seemed paranoid, his attitude toward me was nearly as aggressive when it came to me and my family fraternizing with Haitians at our home, or anywhere on the grounds. This prejudiced attitude was a great concern, and it pushed the two of us closer to confrontation.

That's part of the reason he and I eventually locked horns. I invited Haitians to my house; and in the evenings, Fred and I would visit the VSN in their office by the gate to the compound, and we'd witness to them. In spite of gro chef's vocal opposition, I chose to continue fellowshipping with the locals daily. It was a choice to love, not to rebel. Although love itself can be rebellious when times are evil.

***

Dolores was sick for about a week, saying, "This is really going to be a challenge here. If we stay it will only be with God's help." She was still feeling under the weather on our seventh wedding anniversary on June 24, 1967. Thankfully she felt better on Sunday when we all went to church and Sunday school. It was quite tiring and boring, because we couldn't understand anything being said.

After a week in Haiti, Dolores and I were so exhausted that we talked about going back home. We were so blue not having any pastime and no place to go but to work every day.

***

We were working very hard piping water to all of the houses and the spigot at the main road in Borel. We had to rewire all of the houses for electric because the wiring had been stripped out of every house. We also had to run water to all of the houses and then put in plumbing fixtures, because everything had been removed from the houses. We had to run new power lines because there were no main lines left on the compound. The destruction was caused by the many times the area was ransacked and looted by people—starving people who had no hopeful future in a land ruled by chaos.

Only the Lord was keeping us here.

***

I had not been out of the Artibonite Valley since the night we first arrived, yet one day gro chef sent me to Port-au-Prince with a shopping list, and no interpreter. I was to take the mission pickup truck and go by myself.

This was an overwhelming task as Port-au-Prince is a major city and its streets are not lined with department stores or grocery stores like in the States. Rather, there are different markets and vendors for every need. Unable to speak Creole, I would not have been able to purchase anything on the list. And, I didn't know the way to Port-au-Prince—was only there once when we landed at the airport, and that was after dark.

Fortunately, Pastor Joseph offered to accompany me and interpret for me. It was a long shopping list, and a long day. I was grateful for my new friend's help.

***

After about three weeks, gro chef and I attended a church about an hour's drive away. There were refreshments after church in a Haitian hut. That was quite an experience. We've received mail from our pastor back home, Dolores's sister and her brothers. We welcomed the news from our friends and family.

That same week we drove to the customs area at Port-au-Prince to get the belongings we had shipped in barrels as well as furniture. What a chore. We bought a refrigerator and had it delivered to Borel with our barrels and furniture. Gro chef sent the invoice to the treasurer of the

Commission on World Missions and collected from them the sum I had paid for the refrigerator in Port-au-Prince.

The evening of July 4, we went to Granny's, one of the oldest missions in Haiti at Kenscoff, for a celebration and fireworks. We stayed overnight there, even though Port-au-Prince sure gave us the creeps. Jeff was homesick during the night and wanted to go back to Pennsylvania. Dolores and I didn't blame him one bit.

***

Our first month in Haiti had its share of difficulties—the second was more of the same.

***

I eventually became more comfortable navigating my way around Haiti. I would later discover, that for a few quarters or dollars I could easily hire a local to guide me and interpret for me with the vendors. Haitian motorists will often pick up hitchhikers or tourists walking along the road,
Likewise, it's possible to hire a local to help you shop or interpret for you in exchange for *gourde,* the Haitian currency. Due to a long history of corrupt military governments, funds rarely flow from the state to the people of Haiti. Tourists and missionaries aware of the disastrous economic state of the country are happy to make these monetary trades.

Although I was learning the ropes of our new homeland, even in the first month I had a sinking feeling that something wasn't quite right. Fortunately, some familiar faces from back home would soon be on the way to visit us, and hopefully lift those feelings.

> *Obey those who rule over you, and be submissive, for they watch out for your souls, as those who must give account. Let them do so with joy and not with grief, for that would be unprofitable for you* (Hebrews 13:17 NKJV).

***

Toward the middle of July, we helped gro chef and his family move to Borel. They moved into a very nice remodeled home.

When our pastor and his wife from Pennsylvania arrived for a visit, we were overjoyed. The pastor's wife helped Dolores unpack our barrels and sort through familiar belongings. Then the visit went downhill quickly.

First, the wheel bearing went out on our Rambler car. Our son Jeff developed sores all over his body that lasted a week. Dolores took him to the doctor twice; we were so worried. Then we all were sick with dysentery. I was so sick I had to go to the hospital for relief.

We had to put our trust in the Lord—day by day and moment by moment.

The pastor and his wife stayed for one week; when I took them to the airport, it seemed as we should return to the States with them. Their visit was a needed breath of fresh, familiar air. We spent the whole day in port until Fred and Nancy arrived at the airport. We were so very happy to see them. We stayed that night at the Plaza Hotel—a welcomed change of scenery.

With our travel agent Pierre Allen's help we got our visas at the American Embassy. A highlight was eating at the snack bar at the embassy—it was just like we were eating back in the States, which boosted our morale a bit.

The end of August brought exciting news—Dolores was expecting our second baby.

***

Every morning, Felix arrived at our house and waited on the porch for me to start the day. We drove the mission truck to run errands, usually to pick up rice or lumber. After the fence was built around the property line of Project Help's compound, work began immediately on remodeling a house on the property.

Work on the school buildings was complete enough to begin classes that fall, and Dolores became very involved in the school programs, including the preparation of the school lunches.

After a trip to the States, gro chef and his family returned to Haiti. We couldn't help feeling there was something not quite right when we helped the gro chef and his family move into a newly remodeled home with air conditioning, while all the others were living in shacks.

Not long after gro chef moved out of the Albert Schweitzer property at Deschapelles, the government came and kicked us and Fred and Nancy out of our house. Dolores and Jeff were at the house with Nancy, while Fred and I were in the field. A group of soldiers, most likely Tonton Macoutes[1], showed up at the home in the middle of the day, demanding them to leave the premises. The soldiers said those were government buildings and we had no right to be there.

We had no place to go.

Dolores's brother and his wife—Fred and Nancy—moved into the house in Borel that was still being remodeled, and partially finished. Dolores and Jeff would go back to Pennsylvania. I stayed with Fred and Nancy until the second house was repaired for me and my family, when they returned. That was the plan, at least. But I would be leaving a little sooner than later.

***

In October, a group from the CGGC missions board, including Dolores's father, arrived in Haiti. I gave them a tour of Project Help. With them were men from the States and a man from another denomination who supplied Haiti's missions with a variety of needed equipment.

A maternity nurse at the Albert Schweitzer hospital strongly urged Dolores to have our child back in the States. She needed better medical care. Dolores was eventually ordered home by Albert Schweitzer Hospital, recommending further medical care.

Gro chef, however, said no. Using his position as director, he tried to prevent Dolores from leaving Haiti. But because the CGGC mission board just so happened to be in Haiti at that time, a decision was reached to send Dolores and Jeff back to the U.S., regardless of gro chef's disapproval.

At the end of October, Dolores and Jeff boarded the jet for home. I believe if it hadn't been for the Lord giving me strength I would have departed also. Fred, Nancy, and I set off for Borel that afternoon. I'm glad they were with me—it was a hard parting. We also took Randy and his family along back to Borel with us. He was a Mennonite from the Midwest and his wife had gone home to have her baby and was now returning to Haiti.

I was homesick without Dolores and Jeff; I was lonely. It was a great change for me to be without my wife and son. I worked on the house and wrote letters to send home. I thought of the boys over in Vietnam with no family, facing life-and-death situations every day. It was slight comfort knowing that my family was safe in the States.

Note

1. Tonton Macoutes were armed men known for corruption and brutality in Haiti; also known as MVSN.

****

5
Tension and Turmoil

It was becoming increasingly clear to many at Project Help that their gro chef was doing some unnecessary spending. Some of what we were told to do didn't make sense. Everyone else was wrong and gro chef was always right. He had ways of justifying unjustifiable behavior.

Tension and suspicion mounted when I discovered that he was requesting that any and all monetary donations go directly to him. Checks were to be written in his name, not Project Help, insisting that denominations and other organizations could not have a bank account in Haiti. All accounts had to be under an individual's name.

Occasionally gro chef rented a large vacation villa for his family in the mountains above Port-au-Prince; even though there was a mission just down the road that was run by Granny that would rent out a nice house for travelers and their families at very inexpensive rates.

I saw the villa once and was astonished. I wondered if the denomination knew that some of their donations were going to fund extravagances like this. Gro chef may have sensed my discomfort with the place, as I was never invited back. I wasn't in Haiti to be on vacation—I was there to accomplish something meaningful and purposeful for God.

***

In the fall of 1967, after gro chef had lived in the remodeled home for only a few months, word began going around that construction was to begin on a second house for him and his family.

By now, I, the timid farmer from Pennsylvania, was beginning to feel a righteous indignation welling up inside. We had put in sinks, countertops, showers, commodes; we painted, installed lights, air conditioning, everything a comfortable home could have—yet in a matter of months gro chef started building another new house for himself. It was almost more than I could swallow.

Our houses and the other buildings for Project Help were of no concern to the director. Combined with his aggressive manner and prejudice attitude toward the Haitians, gro chef's demeanor had become so unbearable that I simply could not keep quiet. I'm not exactly certain what initially began the confrontation, but it began with a simple unwillingness to participate in the construction of the second house. There were other projects on the compound that needed attention.

When I confronted him about the finances, he said I didn't understand or know what was going on. He was a hard guy to confront because he had the answer to everything. He believed that he knew everything and was never wrong because he had been in the military. And if anyone questioned him, they got nowhere.

Nevertheless, I often questioned gro chef's approach to doing things—like installing commodes without a wax seal, and instead using cement. Then smashing the commode when it broke and replacing it, rather than fixing it; or wiring buildings with electricity but with no ground wire. His typical response to any questioning of his decisions was often a barrage of disrespect and gaslighting. Many Haitians and Americans alike experienced that response from him. His bombast and temper more than made up for the absence of anyone else's presence around the compound. Soon others in Borel would grow weary of his behavior, and begin to distance themselves. Much worse was how the gro chef spent money indiscriminately—money sent to Haiti by faithful Christian servants. He decided he needed a second house for him and his family. At that point Dolores and I didn't even have a place of our own.

> *Do all things without grumbling or disputing, that you may be blameless and innocent, children of God without blemish in the midst of a crooked and twisted generation, among whom you shine as lights in the world, holding fast to the word of life, so that in the day of Christ I may be proud that I did not run in vain or labor in vain* (Philippians 1:14-16).

There was still a lot of building going on at Project Help in November 1967 during the warm autumn and winter months in the Caribbean. Work teams from various denominations would fly in for a couple of weeks at a time to help with construction. While working on the second house and evangelizing, my in-laws and I kept busy re-wiring and preparing other buildings for use as schools, church, and so forth. Most of the buildings in Haiti didn't have indoor plumbing or electricity.

We started using cement blocks for walls and trussed roofs with tin roofs, which became a common practice for most missions. But many Haitians still don't have a cement block house or a metal roof. These days we try to meet the standard for hurricane proof; but even as this portion of the book is being written, an earthquake hit Haiti and more than 2,000 people were killed and tens of thousands are homeless.[1] Unfortunately, Haiti had and still has many complex issues when it comes to the basics of life.

***

Haiti's bad reputation concerning voodoo is rampant worldwide. What disturbs me most about this is hearing Christians and missionaries and pastors make comments such as, "Well, nothing can be done in Haiti. They're all sold out to the devil. They made a pact with the devil when they started the revolution. They're not interested in the Gospel. They're demon-possessed people." None of that is true! But it is propagated by the majority of Christians and Christian leaders.

If it was truly that way throughout the country, work teams wouldn't have felt safe going into the mountains and sleeping out in the open, which they did on many occasions. We started churches and invited the people to come—and people came.

Contrary to some people, the Haitians don't have a "whites are devils" mindset. They're not prejudiced or biased. They have some hang-ups and problems, but so does every culture in every country. Many Haitians, in fact, migrate to the United States and Canada and Europe. And if they felt we were some kind of evil devils, they wouldn't want to live in countries where the majority of the population are white. Haitians are on the whole friendly and eager to hear what you have to say.

Regarding voodoo (also spelled vodou), a common saying is that Haitians are 70 percent Catholic, 30 percent Protestant, and 100 percent voodoo. That was an overstatement. Haitians who are not Christians will defend voodoo and its tenants. But voodoo is not what most think it is. An interesting article can be found on the *National Geographic.com* website.[2] And most people in Haiti who embrace Christ will denounce voodoo and give a public testimony in church, asking the pastor to publicly baptize them—they also will burn all of the voodoo artifacts they may have. To them, you're either a Christian or you're not. And if you're a Christian, you stop all the voodoo rituals.

***

A personal story about such things: One of the last times I went back to Haiti was with Jeff to see if a site was ready to build a new church. They were digging the footers on a piece of land that was not beside the old church. I said to Jeff, "Why didn't you build beside the old church?"

He said, "Well, it's too steep. So we bought this piece of land which was above the road and was flat."

"Who did you buy the land from?" I asked.

"The man in the house up there on the bank a little ways. We bought it off of him. It was literally in his front yard."

"Yeah? Well that was nice of him," I said.

"Yeah, especially for being a witch doctor!"

So the next month a work team was there building a church on that site.

While going to a church in the mountains one Sunday, a storm blew in and our guide told us to take shelter on a man's porch. The guide and the man started talking. The old guy said of the weather, "It's terrible. It blows our fruit trees down and messes up our cattle and crops and we can't sell them in the market for a reasonable price."

Our guide said to the man—who was a witchdoctor, I found out later—"It's because of you heathen who reject the Lord!" He told him that right to his face while we were sitting there.

As we left, I saw there was a cross in the guy's yard; yet our guide had given him an evangelistic blast like I never heard. Still, he didn't tell us to get off his porch or leave his property. It surely made me wonder.

***

The days are long and lonely since Dolores and Jeff left Haiti. It seems like ages since they left. When you are by yourself, you get to thinking about your life. A man's life is short and full of difficulties. But God has been good to me. When I think of the Haitians, I must be thankful. It is hard to keep from getting homesick. I think of my family and how good we had it—and yet we complained. I think more people could use a mission trip to another country. Then maybe they would have more sympathy and compassion on a lost world.

It is so different here than what we imagined, and we truly need God's help. And so do the Haitians. They are nicer people than I even realized people could be. They are very kind and friendly and have good sense of humor—even during their hard way of life. When I see them hoeing their fields to plant their crops I think of how I grumbled when I had to plow with a tractor and work 16 hours a day.

We hope and pray that something we say and do here will be of help to the people. Most of all spiritually. We tend to forget that while we live in nice houses, half of the world sleeps under a grass roof.

In times like these it may be easy for some Christians to get discouraged; to doubt the plan they believed God had for them, or to think they're being punished.

I never gave the devil much credit for being powerful. Almighty God is my strength.

I learned this chorus from an elderly evangelist before going to Haiti and during many impossible days it inspired me in Haiti:

I'll live for Jesus day after day,
I'll live for Jesus, let come what may;
The Holy Spirit I will obey,
And live for Jesus day after day.

***

If your brother or sister sins, go and point out their fault, just between the two of you. If they listen to you, you have won them over. But if they will not listen, take one or two others along, so that "every matter may be established by the testimony of two or three witnesses." If they still refuse to listen, tell it to the church; and if they refuse to listen even to the church, treat them as you would a pagan or a tax collector (Matthew 18:15-17).

Dolores had been admitted to the hospital immediately upon arriving home. Jeff recovered fully and stayed with Dolores's parents. I made it back to Pennsylvania to be with Dolores and Jeff in time for the holidays. Dolores was in the hospital for several weeks. She went into labor shortly after New Year's Day. On January 4, 1968, Kirby Swope was born. While we were away, Fred continued working on our house so it would be ready by the time we returned in March.

While back in the States, I made it a point to visit a number of churches to present Missions messages to many of the churches that were supporting Project Help. During these visits I noticed some unsettling trends. At every church someone would say something like, "Wasn't it nice that we were able to send you guys that money so you could buy that cow for the Christmas feast?"

I found this question increasingly odd each time it was asked, because I recalled only one time when gro chef hosted a cow roast—with one cow—during our time in Haiti. It was apparent that gro chef was exaggerating in the newsletters he sent back to the States, boasting about his success, and taking credit for projects begun by other pastors. I felt as if a veil of deception had been cast over what was happening in Borel.

Gro chef could explain things in a way that made it look as though he was doing the right thing. I knew if I was going to address this matter biblically, I would need to address gro chef in tandem with another fellow Christian.

It seemed the Lord wasted no time in arranging just such a meeting, the moment my family and I returned to Haiti.

Notes

1. "Haiti's Hunger Crisis Bites Deeper After Devastating quake"; *Reuters,* August 30, 2021; https://www.usnews.com/news/world/articles/2021-08-30/haitis-hunger-crisis-bites-deeper-after-devastating-quake; accessed October 5, 2021.

2. Sharon Guynup, "Haiti: Possessed by Voodoo," July 7, 2004, *National Geographic;* https://www.nationalgeographic.com/culture/article/haiti-ancient-traditions-voodoo; accessed September 9, 2021.

****

6
Strength, Not Fear

A gentle answer turns away wrath, but a harsh word stirs up anger (Proverbs 15:1 NIV).

In March 1968, civil rights protests, led by Martin Luther King Jr., were reaching heated levels. Joe Frazier knocked out Buster Mathis at the new Madison Square Garden in New York City. Country singers Johnny Cash and June Carter were married in Franklin, Kentucky.

Meanwhile, the war in Vietnam raged on with no end in sight, as President Lyndon Johnson's popularity declined. U.S. Senator Robert F. Kennedy of New York, younger brother of the late President John F. Kennedy, entered the race for the Democratic Party presidential nomination challenging U.S. President Johnson at the August 26 national convention.

But all of these events were far from our thoughts as we, now a family of four, prepared to fly back to Haiti together. Once again, François "Papa Doc" Duvalier was being confronted with rebel forces challenging his dictatorship; and before summer's end, the people of Haiti would be under martial law.

In March 1968, we arrived safely in Haiti. When we arrived on the compound, all the school children screamed, "Hello!" We felt so welcomed when we were invited into each classroom and they sang us a song in English; two classrooms even gave us bouquets of flowers. They also had a special service for us at church.

Nancy had our house all ready for us. Boy is it nice to have a place of our own. That month, life returned to "normal" for our family and for Nancy and Fred. A birthday party and cakes, our stove and refrigerator arrived, screens were put on the windows, ice cream parties after church.

The beginning of April, Dolores wrote in her journal that after a Wednesday prayer meeting, she had never been so mixed up in all her life, confessing that only God can straighten things out. Thankfully, our family was happy and healthy; Kirby is three months old now, and such a good baby. Jeff loves school.

***

In Haiti, then and now, house fires were fairly common. Open flames were used regularly for cooking and boiling water. As many homes were made of wood, with rooftops typically made of grass, structure fires were inevitable.

A team of helpers from The Mennonite Central Committee in Pennsylvania arrived and Fred and I took them by horseback into the mountains to take the Gospel to the people, as well as supplies that the Mennonite's brought with them. Riding on a horse was not my thing. I was raised on a farm but not on a horse. Horseback riding on a wooden saddle in the mountains was not for the uninitiated. Though horseback was a common mode of transport in Haiti back then, I felt sorry for the horses and mules. Many of them had open sores on their backs. They weren't very big either, so it was hard for them to carry big Americans. The Mennonite Central Committee had packages to deliver, so I went with them. We journeyed to a church in the mountains that Pastor Jules had planted. Four pastors from Pennsylvania were along with that trip on a work team.

***

There was an ugly stain clouding what should have been a joyous arrival back in Haiti. The moment we set foot on the Project Help compound, gro chef wasted no time letting us know, once again, who was in charge. Dolores and I were berated for a full five hours—mostly ranting, empty threats, excuses, and nonsense.

I read the book of James a lot during that time after returning to Haiti. James made it clear to me that in religion, politics, and reality—there is good and evil. There is true and false. And the only thing I could bank on was knowing that I was trusting the Lord and serving the Lord.

***

By the autumn of 1968, gro chef had alienated Pastor Jules, who had funded and began his ministry before Project Help arrived. Jules was told he had to give Project Help all of his churches, and orphanages, and schools. Pastor Jules declined and left the mission. Pastor Jules was my Creole teacher and although I was sad he left, I understood. We continued to work together on the reverend's various orphanage, churches, and school projects for many years.

Tensions reached a new high between gro chef and I when he told me that men I had helped were probably dead because they didn't have approval to preach in the mountains. I later discovered that no permits were necessary to preach in Haiti, that Haiti has religious freedom, and the people in the mountains welcome Christians. Preaching in the mountains was a common missionary practice in Haiti. Another lie from gro chef.

***

My passion to share the Gospel with people was matched only by my Haitian brethren. I yearned for opportunities to assist the need all around in Haiti. Haiti needs witnesses. I prayed, "Lord, give me boldness to witness to whoever, wherever." Many evenings, Fred and I went to the office of the Tonton Macoute and had conversations with them. They were always open and welcomed our conversations. Men in the field would stop and listen when we shared the Gospel of Jesus with them.

Eventually, as the number of churches in the area began to grow, I began recognizing the faces of people we had witnessed to at the church services and events; even including members of the Tonton Macoute, singing and fellowshipping with the others. I realized we had more to offer the Haitians as a Gospel witness than I ever could have offered as a farmer. There was a lot they could teach me about farming in the tropics. Who they really needed was Christ—He is the One who would make a lasting and eternal change in their lives.

***

I never had any opposition by any practitioner of voodoo. One of the first converts we celebrated at Borel when Project Help officially opened was a local witch doctor. After he became a Christian, he would often come back and I would visit and spend time with him.

Many people in Haiti allowed me the opportunity to share the Gospel with them. Even a neighboring witchdoctor living on the other side of the fence took notice. His young nephew would climb a tree by our house to read books by the light of our porch. Years later this young fellow attended seminary to become a pastor.

Spreading the message of the Gospel in Haiti was our purpose. There wasn't much in the way of media. Haiti had newspapers and some radio, but their abilities to serve evangelistic purposes would be lost on a rural population that was mostly illiterate and without electricity. Reaching them meant getting off of the beaten path.

Several aspects of the Haitian culture were extremely different and difficult to come to terms with. For example, women are subservient to a major degree. And people are so poor and destitute that a woman may not have a house, home, food, or any of the necessities of life. The one way women have a roof over their heads or any necessities is to sleep with some guy who has some means.

When couples got saved and started attending church, they wanted to be married right away.
However, the cultural idea of marriage in Haiti means if you're going to get married, you should already have a job, a house, and so forth. You have to be able to provide for your wife and family. But there is a certain cost for the marriage license, and a cost for the ceremony.

Often times I'd ask a couple when they were getting married, and the answer would be, "Well, when I get enough money," or, "When I get a house."

Due to this cultural tradition, it could sometimes take years for a couple to save up enough funds for a marriage license and a house. At times, ministries like Project Help could assist couples off-set these costs. That was something we would do; to help these couples get a leg up.

As I was growing into a stronger witness for Christ, some of my Haitian friends asked me to speak at their church. At Pastor Joseph's church in the city of Saint Marc, I preached my first sermon.

***

> *"Be strong and courageous. Do not be afraid or terrified because of them, for the Lord your God goes with you; he will never leave you nor forsake you." Then Moses summoned Joshua and said to him in the presence of all Israel, "Be strong and courageous, for you must go with this people into the land that the Lord swore to their ancestors to give them, and you must divide it among them as their inheritance. The Lord himself goes before you and will be with you; he will never leave you nor forsake you. Do not be afraid; do not be discouraged"* (Deuteronomy 31:6-8 NIV).

In June 1968, I read this passage in Deuteronomy 31:6: *"Do not be afraid or terrified because of them, for the Lord your God goes with you: he will never leave you or forsake you."*

That night, little did my family or I know that we would soon be face to face with soldiers, be forced to answer accusatory questions, and be packing up our suitcases with necessities before night's end, in case things took a turn for the worse.

One of the pastors in Borel was in charge of enrolling children in school. He would announce in church that enrollment was full. But when parents went to him and asked what they could do to get their child in school, he gave them a price. Because bribery was such a common way of life in Haiti, parents knew that if they wanted their child to get an education, they would have to give something in return.

Felix Latonda and many locals appreciated Project Help and the pastors and the good things they were doing in Borel. They did not want to see corruption take over the church the way it had in their government. Felix told me, "We know what you guys are doing and you're helping the Haitian people. But that one pastor is bleeding them for all he can get."

According to Felix, the Tonton Macoutes did not like having some brazen pastor encroaching on their turf. Such bribery and abuses may be commonplace among the military, but they didn't care for competition from civilians. I think the Tonton in that area hear all kinds of accusations and stories; Haiti is crooked and corrupt, and they don't want anyone but them doing it.

The soldiers temporarily commandeered the mission's truck to transport the prisoner to Saint Marc. Fred was asked to drive some of the soldiers, along with the pastor, to the prison there. Later, as my brother-in-law was transporting the soldiers back to the compound, one of the men informed him they would be searching everyone's home immediately upon their return.

They came back to our compound at Borel and searched all of our houses trying to find a radio transmitter. They searched to no avail.

Fred had given the heads up to Dolores and me, but we did not seem to be top suspects. Our houses were the last buildings to be searched, and our wives had hot meals ready to share with them when they arrived.

The Tonton Macoute were unable to locate a radio transmitter, or any evidence of rebellion within the village. However, they had taken one of their pastors—and it was not expected he would ever be seen alive again.

That night, the commandant of the region asked me if I could drive him to Port-au-Prince in the morning. I, of course, obliged. Being an army officer, he was able to get through all of the roadblocks on the road to Port-au-Prince, making for a relatively swift and smooth journey. At one point the men stopped at the prison in Saint Mark to see if they could visit the pastor who had been caught in corruption. He was not the haughty, arrogant man I had known previously. He looked more defeated than I had ever seen him.

Although we were never ejected from our home for a second time, it wouldn't be long before circumstances finally forced us out of the country once again.

***

Our second departure from Haiti came swiftly and unexpectedly—all within a few chaotic weeks.

On May 20, 1968, I went to Port-au-Prince to pick up mail and heard explosions from planes flying overhead bombing the city and targeting the palace. As I drove past the palace we saw armed Tonton Macoute soldiers jumping on trucks and mounting guns before heading out from the palace.

When I reached the Hotel Plaza where we received our mail, I was told that the rebels took over the airport at Cap-Haitien and also the radio station operated by Oriental Mission Society (OMS).

The rebels expected the city's residents to give them a warm welcome. Instead, they implored them to leave the city. As the rebels quickly flew away, a coast guard cutter and other militia began firing upon them.

The whole country was put under martial law—I could not travel back to Borel for a week. I had to retrieve government papers from one of top officials at the VSN to return to Borel. It was the only time since coming face-to-face with "Papa Doc" that I had any encounters with a top Haitian government official.

I prayed about what to do—to awaken one morning to perfect peace. Although I eventually returned to Borel, perfect peace would have to wait.

The events of May 20 created such an uproar that by early June, the American Embassy informed us that we were to take ourselves and our two young children back to the United States right away. By the end of June, we were back in Pennsylvania.

I was far more devastated about leaving Haiti than I was about leaving home. I was heartsick about leaving Haiti, and the Haitian people.

As difficult as things had been while in Haiti, this is where I felt I belonged. But this was not the time. A close look at biblical Scripture reveals how, oftentimes, those who seek a closer walk with God must venture into the wilderness first, to be tested.

Never did I imagine the wilderness would be in my own homeland.

****

Part II
Back Home

Beloved, do not believe every spirit, but test the spirits, whether they are of God; because many false prophets have gone out into the world*. By this you know the Spirit of God:* ***Every spirit that confesses that Jesus Christ has come in the flesh is of God****, and every spirit that does not confess that Jesus Christ has come in the flesh is not of God. And this is the spirit of the Antichrist, which you have heard was coming, and is now already in the world. You are of God, little children, and have overcome them, because* ***He who is in you is greater than he who is in the world.***
(1 John 4:1-4 NKJV)

****

7
Closed Doors and Opened Windows

So do not be ashamed of the testimony about our Lord or of me his prisoner. Rather, join with me in suffering for the gospel, by the power of God (2 Timothy 1:8 NIV).

After the United States embassy in Port-au-Prince sent my family and I back to the States for safety's sake, I soon learned that gro chef had spoken untruths to the Commission on World Missions about me, making it nearly impossible for me to serve on any other mission, in Haiti or elsewhere. I was stunned that the Commission was allowing a wolf to roam freely among the flock.

I thought of Judas Iscariot and the fact that nothing can thwart the plans of God. God can even use attempts against His will to fulfill His purpose. Nevertheless, this was a personal reality check, and only the beginning of sorrows that would come to me by way of the church itself.

Up to this point, I had an idealized vision of what Christian leaders should be. I was learning the harsh truth that those in the church can be as flawed and unreliable as anyone else. He saw that, unfortunately, the church can be just as naive, at times, as any other group of people. Once they realize they've been duped, they don't want to talk about it.

Unable to get reassigned, I had little choice but to carry on God's work at home—my surrounding area would be my mission field. It would have been easy for me to feel destined to live a life of thankless unappreciation for my services, both to God and humanity. But I refused to be deterred, even in the face of the most destructive of all spiritual weapons—discouragement. I knew that I knew that God would never leave or forsake me, because the Bible says clearly says so:

> *Do not be afraid or discouraged, for the Lord will personally go ahead of you. He will be with you; he will neither fail you nor abandon you* (Deuteronomy 31:8 NLT; see also Joshua 1:5; Hebrews 13:5;).

I continued to put my trust in the Lord, although not sure what was next. I took a job working as plumber for a time, while Dolores, Jeff, and Kirby stayed with her parents.

***

In September 1969, my next divine assignment came my way, although not in the form of another mission trip.

During the time I was working away from home, I was contacted about being the pastor for the five churches on the Walnut Grove charge. The pastor at my home church was retiring, and he recommended me as a lay pastor. This would not be a small task, as the call entailed pastoring five sibling churches in Southern Huntingdon County as well. Nevertheless, a door had clearly opened for me. Facing this decision drove me deep into prayer. I remember the nights of praying and telling God how scared I was, and asking if I was the right man to go there. It was a real struggle trying to decide. Dolores and I sought God together.

I had never attended college or seminary and had no academic preparation for pastoral ministry. I did some minimal guest preaching in Saint Marc, but it was overwhelming to imagine preaching at five separate church services every week, including the responsibility of counseling, conducting funerals and weddings, facilitating church meetings and Bible studies, door-to-door evangelism, and many other aspects of the church.

But God—God doesn't always call on those who seem the most qualified. But God *does* qualify those He calls. Knowing this basic truth of Christian theology, I stepped out in faith and up to the task in spite of seemingly being unprepared.

It was quite a chore to study the courses and pastor five churches at the same time. I pastored in the daytime and studied a correspondence course and ministerial training program at night. On one Sunday, I would preach three church services; and on alternate Sundays, I pastored the two largest churches. I would go for church and Sunday School at one church, and in the evening go to the other one. I also had prayer meetings and other services.

Between serving as a lay pastor and earning my minister's license, I finished an eight to nine year course in six years, while pastoring the five Walnut Grove churches. We had moved into a parsonage, a house owned by the denomination.

I farmed part-time for my dad on Saturdays. When I felt overwhelmed, a pastor by the name of Cornelius agreed to fill in. He eventually took over two of the five Walnut Grove churches after I consolidated to Cherry Grove before moving to another church community altogether by the end of the 1970s.

***

Life in the 1970s brought the celebration of the birth of two more sons: Kevin in 1970 and Jamie in 1975. Death also knocked on our family door as both of my grandmothers passed; Dad's mom in the early '70s and my mother's mom in 1976.

Back in Haiti, Project Help continued to grow. I felt encouraged to go back when I learned gro chef was no longer affiliated with the organization. I eventually went back to Haiti, taking numerous church mission groups. But as troubling and challenging as mission work had already proven to be, evangelism at home would prove to be an even more frustrating challenge.

***

In April 1971, the notorious Haitian dictator and self-appointed President for Life, Francois "Papa Doc" Duvalier, died a week after his 64th birthday. Knowing his days were few, Duvalier appointed his 19-year-old son, Jean-Claude to succeed him. Retaining the title of President for Life, the younger Duvalier, known as "Baby Doc," introduced superficial changes to his father's corrupt regime. The remaining members of the Duvalier family would live lives of extravagance at the expense of the Haitian people, exceeding even Papa Doc's pilfering of millions from the national treasury. Baby Doc amassed a wealth of about $600 million while the Haitian people were some of the poorest people in the world.

When Duvalier died and Baby Doc took over, it was kind of open-season for all the Tonton Macoute. Many of the people I knew, after we left Haiti, were either killed or went into hiding.

In spite of the obvious corruption still lingering within Haiti's government, the county would be relatively safe once again for travelers and missionaries. Although Baby Doc kept his father's Tonton Macoute, now officially titled the "Volontaires de la Securite Nationale" (VSN) any of the more terrifying elements of Papa Doc's regime were done away with, making the 1970s a relatively peaceful decade.

***

The first two times I lived in Haiti, I was a permanent resident. It was usual for missionaries to be in the mission field for four or five years. Our intent was for life; we had packed for the first five years. Now with a full time role as a pastor in the U.S., a residency in Haiti seemed unlikely. Nevertheless, I purposed to return as often as possible, if even for only a matter of weeks or days at a time.

I coordinated with Pastor Jules and my brother-in-law, Fred, setting up trips for various projects. I would round up teams to take to Haiti, where we would typically work on building projects for churches, schools, and orphanages.

These trips almost felt like vacations compared to the stress and turmoil of pastoring five churches in rural Pennsylvania. I discovered that evangelizing to impoverished Haitians was incredibly easy compared to evangelizing to privileged, comfortable Americans.

The life-changing impact I saw taking place in the lives of Haitian people by simply sharing the Word of God with them was nothing short of miraculous; especially when contrasted to the entitled stubbornness of many Americans. Few in America had a thirst for the Gospel as the people of Haiti. It would seem the American mindset was much tougher to crack. This was an unsettling reality awareness that I may not have detected had I not evangelized first to the destitute citizens of Haiti before doing likewise in the States.

***

For God has not given us the spirit of fear, but of power and of love and of a sound mind (2 Timothy 1:7 NKJV).

I took up journaling again in 1973 as a close friend said it may be therapeutic to write my thoughts and emotions. The following entries are raw and real—from the end of August to the end of December, I share with you my writings, not to brag or with false humility, but with an authentic yearning to reveal the heart and mind of a missionary-turned-pastor who had to work daily at being the man God intended—for myself, my family, my parishioners, and for Him.

August 27, 1973
Prayed for a great day. Seemed so long since I shared the Gospel. So I prayed for the opportunity. TR had already responded to "Four Laws," so I prayed to thank Christ for coming into his life. When I left, GK was standing at his door and wanted me to talk with him about God's love and forgiveness. Men are hungry for God.

August 28, 1973
Prayed for guidance for last message at New Granada Church of God. Spoke on the Gospel. (Matthew 28). Was given a great farewell. They loved the Word and never hindered the preaching of the Word. They thanked me for sharing the Word and I thanked them for their faithfulness.

August 29, 1973
I was somewhat apprehensive about the service at Walnut Grove Church of God.

August 30, 1973
I have a new task to face at Cherry Grove Church of God; feeling a great challenge and a huge sense of inadequacy to the need there.

August 31, 1973
Somewhat troubled, but Cherry Grove Church of God responded to the challenge; end of Walnut Grove charge. "Oh you of little faith." I really didn't believe a year ago that I would see this day, or be the pastor of Cherry Grove Church of God.

September 1, 1973
I needed a second message for Cherry Grove Church of God; God supplied abundantly. Four years ago when I was called to Walnut Grove Church of God charge, I told God if He would give me one sermon, I would go; He never failed to supply every message in almost four years. Totaling about 823 messages, plus funerals.

September 3, 1973
Labor Day – God provided a way to get the power saw chain for Fred in Haiti. I took it to Bailey to take tomorrow to Haiti. God really cares and provides.

October 15, 1973
It seems like God has to deal with me so often. I get distressed and depressed when I fail to trust Him for complete guidance. Oh, to be close and in fellowship with Jesus, and to trust Him to guide in all things, especially to guide me in witnessing. It appears that the devil does more to scare me in regard to telling men about Christ than any place else. We are burdened for the possibilities of more problems in the work in Haiti. Oh God, call and send men to Haiti who will honor You and bring glory to Your name. Lord, send forth laborers; they are needed.

Had a great day in the Word this past Sunday; studied Israel in Promise from Genesis, Isaiah and Jeremiah in prophecy, in current history and war. How great God is to restore Israel after 2,500 years and to make them victorious over 60,000,000 Arabians.

It seems so hard for people to give themselves to witnessing. Success in witnessing is sharing Christ in the power of the Holy Spirit, and leaving the results to God. Now, if I could only do this in regard to the church, and as well my concern for our mission work in Haiti. Lord, it is so good to trust You for everything, even for those You have prepared for us to witness to this evening.

October 19, 1973
Felt very disturbed and depressed. It seems I am so far from a close relationship with the Lord. I tried all week to prepare a message from II Corinthians. I have completed through chapter 7:1, with revival coming. I guess I will go to some other Scripture and then it seems to be that so little is happening when I go visiting. I guess I am trying to do too much

and not trusting in the Lord enough. When I am trying, I am not trusting. But revival is coming, and so many are unconcerned. Oh what sin in the church, and what terrible sin people in the community commit.

November 20, 1973
We had revival on November 4th through 11th, the Lord called two more to discipleship in preparation for witnessing. Oh, to learn to trust in the Lord to work all things out. I really trusted Him to prepare me last week. He dealt with those things in my life that were a hindrance; as He filled or controlled me as I trusted Him.

We had a good response at Six Mile Run Revival on Friday evening and then what a good time I had at camp. It is good to be in the study this morning and expect the Lord to prepare me for this week. Oh, the wonders of preaching the message of the Lord and seeing the Holy Spirit move people to confession or salvation. Dolores and I long to trust the Lord in everything.

December 3, 1973
I had a great time studying "How to be filled with the Holy Spirit." Witnessing class was so hard; it seemed we were not directed by the Holy Spirit.

December 7, 1973
Victory. Was a hard week. Accomplished nothing from my point of view. One person has been so disgruntled with the church and has brought a burden to everyone, council agrees to pray, could not study or prepare today. I could not pray; the heavens seemed like brass, the Holy Spirit prevailed; my burden is lifted and just finished my fourth sermon outline this evening. Oh, the power of God that is available. I trust Him to direct election Sunday.

December 26, 1973
More things are wrought by prayer than this world can dream of. The Lord has sure directed in the work of the church, and in our lives. I trust Him to direct His work in this coming year in the church at Cherry Grove Church. Oh, what things the Lord has wrought this year. It is thrilling to trust Him for what He will bring to pass in 1974. Romans 8:28, we know He loves us and whatever He brings to pass will be for our good. Lord,

help me to commit myself to You, totally in 1974. Whatever You have in store for me; recognizing Your priority on my life.

****

8
Season of Silence

Jesus went through all the towns and villages, teaching in their synagogues, proclaiming the good news of the kingdom and healing every disease and sickness. When he saw the crowds, he had compassion on them, because they were harassed and helpless, like sheep without a shepherd. Then he said to his disciples, "The harvest is plentiful but the workers are few. Ask the Lord of the harvest, therefore, to send out workers into his harvest field" (Matthew 9:35-38 NIV).

Pray for workers, but don't have any reservations about who God sends.

I was in my element when I was sharing the Good News of salvation with hungry souls. Whether in Haiti or in my own back yard, so to speak, in Pennsylvania, I knew there was work to be done in the harvest field.

I often worked to raise support for a number of projects, not all were associated with Project Help. Pastor Jules was still planting churches and was in need of buildings. When not thinking about and planning efforts geared toward Haiti, I was involved with my own local flock. When you are a pastor, you see all kinds of sin that needs to be confronted with the Gospel of Jesus.

There was one man in the congregation who seemed perpetually disgruntled and spread rumors based on any grievance he perceived, real or imagined. He would make up negative and false stories. When the elders would track the stories down, there was no truth to any of them. He eventually went to another church and took a few people with him; he did the same kind of things in that church, till he finally drove the pastor out.

These are not new problems in the church. It's as old as the church itself. Indeed, the Bible warns of these very problems and of those who spread discord among the brethren. Ask most faithful Christians and many will tell you that the biggest threat facing the church is from within. The apostle Paul wrote of this:

> *For I am afraid that when I come I may not find you as I want you to be, and you may not find me as you want me to be. I fear*

> *that there may be discord, jealousy, fits of rage, selfish ambition, slander, gossip, arrogance and disorder. I am afraid that when I come again my God will humble me before you, and I will be grieved over many who have sinned earlier and have not repented...* (2 Corinthians 12:20-21 NIV).

These stresses were taking a toll on my emotional well-being. Fortunately, there was always Haiti to look forward to—a land of such beauty and sadness, but also a place where the Gospel is welcomed and taken seriously. The reward of serving in this place, of being able to let God's light shine so others may be blessed brought tremendous encouragement.

In November, we had a successful revival service at Six Mile Run, a neighboring church in the mountains near Cherry Grove. I often preached revival and evangelistic services as a guest pastor at other churches, as well as in my churches. In spite of the victories, I struggled to know God's will, and battled perfectionism and self-criticism.

Nevertheless, I purposed every day to keep trusting the Lord and stand wholeheartedly on the promises of God. I knew that if I continued to walk out a life of obedience and faithfulness, my emotions were of no concern.

It is the fervent belief of any Christian who has determined within themselves to endure to the end, they must be someone of prayer. It seems to be easy as a pastor to get to trusting your own wisdom and think you have the answers. It is something else to commit our ideas to the Lord, and then ask His will to be done. Sometimes we get carried away with our own agenda and thought, rather than confessing our sin and trusting the Holy Spirit to guide our lives in fulfilling the Great Commission.

***

I began 1974 with the Lord impressing upon me to fulfill the Great Commission. I believe that there is little use in me going on living if I am not a witness to the saving grace of God. This is why I was born—to share the Gospel. As proof of God's enduring compassion for His children, we are still seeing the results of the witness program (Campus

Crusade for Christ) that began a year ago. Many people are responding—people who seemed unmoved when witnessed to. It takes time for some people to yield to the conviction of the Holy Spirit. Even people who have given up on witnessing for the Lord are given no rest. Paul wrote, *"Woe is unto me, if I preach not the gospel!"* (1 Corinthians 9:16 KJV).

During the summer of 1974 I wrote that I have been afraid to witness. I had so many random thoughts going through my head! Some include: I am afraid of defeat. I am afraid to preach for fear people will reject God's message. I can't face defeat. Where is the obedience of the cross? What will I tell God, if I don't preach? My duty is to preach the Gospel; His duty is to produce the results. It is not what I have; it is Who has me. To worry about men is to seek their applause.

Love for Christ is the only motive for service. Do I trust God or men? Why do I worry about being accepted by men? When God has accepted me, forgiven me and saved me. Does God expect as much of me as I do? Why worry about what people think, does God think the same way? Why worry about what I don't get done, does God bring the results or do I? Why worry about people? Does God accept them as they are? Why be dissatisfied with myself, would God forgive me, then be dissatisfied with me? To think Jesus would accept me, just as I am is the most amazing thought.

Upon returning from Haiti in July, while praying I came to this realization, "Oh, Lord, how often have I wanted to be something, to do something, to be outstanding or great? How humiliating; yet how true, I am nothing, worthless, only a sinner saved by grace. Apart from Christ, what would I be? It is very discomforting to face up to what I could have become apart from Christ's control in my life. Oh, Jesus whatever the cost, wherever it takes me, I am Yours!" Oh, the peace that came when all was committed to Christ.

In September I began to think ahead to the new year. I desired to know God better—not only by Bible reading and prayer, but by letting God speak to me and direct my life. I desire to be more like Christ in being loving and patient. I want to develop boldness in witnessing and overcome the trait of taking things in my own hands—therefore worrying rather than trusting. I believe that I will be more effective if I let God be in control, rather than continually trying to run my own life. God answered our prayers for Kevin who was having health issues—all his tests were negative!

***

Bouts of depression overwhelm me and I sometimes wonder if I am worth anything to the Lord; I seem to be a worthless servant. Yet I know that I know Christ died for me, saved me, redeemed me, called me and used me. Yes! I can see a wide open door of opportunity and responsibility open to me. It is ready for me to enter by an adventure in faith. My attitude is hindering me, not God's attitude about me. I feel so unfit to serve the Lord and that hinders me from being used of God in Cherry Grove Church of God, Bangladesh, or Venezuela. I cannot be fit by feelings—I am fit by faith. *"I can do all things through Christ who strengthens me,"* (Philippians 4:13 NKJV) by faith.

Here I am, Lord, feeling controlled by Your power by faith in Jesus Christ. Lord, it is Your will that I enter these wide open doors of opportunity! A year from now, I would like to be completely dependent on Christ to guide my life. I desire to be a witness and to train disciples for Christ who can share their love for You in a powerful way.

My vision for the church is to see everyone sharing Christ in this community. If I leave nothing else to the church, I hope to leave the goal of fulfilling the Great Commission in our day. I believe that the main goal of the church is to train reproducers. Who can train others to be reproducers?

In November we had a good Missionary Convention with Oriental Missionary Society (OMS). I have come to the place where I am not frustrated about whether we should go back to the field, what we should do, or where we should go. I have said, "Yes" to Christ. I am His, and under His control, available to His command, and willing to receive His Commission wherever, whenever, however He desires to use me. Until then I will serve here, knowing He called me here, and has not opened the way to serve anywhere else.

Oh, the wonder of the Lord, to direct us and empower us. Had a very good day today; great service and the congregational meeting was productive. God's desire is to have victories in the battles against the world, the flesh, and the devil. Just trust Him to meet the needs of those who are not right with the Lord. How I need His direction as I face another week, sermons and visits that need to be made.

As I neared the end of my seminary courses and our fourth son entered the world, I wondered what God had next for us.

****

9
New Year, New Beginnings

Now this is the confidence that we have in Him, that if we ask anything according to His will, He hears us (1 John 5:14 NKJV).

My 1975 New Year's Prayer:

Lord, open the way, prepare me, send me, and use me. Lord, help me to live each day in the power of Your Holy Spirit. Help me not to be frustrated because of the past or anxious about the future—but to live in the present in the fullness of the Spirit, trusting You for everything. Lord, You know how small my faith and how great the need; how hard it is for me to trust You in everything. Lord, You know my struggle every time I attempt to do anything; the fear of failure that causes me to think I cannot, the fear of criticism, the feeling others can do it better. Lord, please help me to realize that You never call me to do anything that You don't supply every one of my needs.

Lord, more than anything else, I need perfect trust. Lord, help me to keep the goal in mind. The goal of fulfilling the vision of training more disciples at home, and encouraging the work of fulfilling the Great Commission in Haiti. Lord, I am trusting in You to increase the tape ministry of making disciples in Haiti.

Thank You, Lord. Thanks for the invitation to speak at Stone Glen on Haiti. Thanks for the opportunity to share my ideas with the lay supply and licensed pastors, and to share the missions ministry. Thanks for the discipleship training with other pastors at the pastors' conference at Winebrenner Seminary.

Thank You, Lord, for the first home Bible Study with four persons present this morning. Thanks for the mission goal of $1,000 for Spring Rally. Thank You for the message on forgiveness yesterday and for the help it was to one person—maybe many more. Please God, whatever it takes to reach my brother for You. Thank You, Lord, for Your forgiveness and the therapy from the pastors' conference. Lord, use me today.

***

The new year began with some trepidation and excitement for what 1975 might bring. I was hopeful for a new ministry program by Campus Crusade for Christ that was available on cassette tapes. The usefulness as ministry tools for mission workers in Haiti was fruitful, so I regularly sent tapes.

I often spoke at various churches within the denomination about the work taking place in Haiti. These were opportunities to share missions ideas I had with other pastors. At the annual conference at Winebrenner Seminary of the Churches of God General Conference, I enjoyed the opportunity to pick the brains of pastors and share ideas for missions. In 1975 I was asked to go to Haiti on behalf of Winebrenner to share the program I was using with Campus Crusade for Christ.

***

Ike was a World War II veteran. His brother had been killed in the same region where Ike had been fighting. That experience affected him ever after, and planted a root of bitterness that grew worse over time. In later years he became an alcoholic. When he got sick, he was admitted to the Veterans Hospital in Altoona, Pennsylvania.

Junior was a man from the same community and was close friends with Ike. Two years earlier, Junior knocked at our door in the middle of the night after experiencing a personal tragedy. He accepted Christ that night, and was delivered from alcoholism.

Junior and Ike had been drinking buddies. This was a couple of years before Ike's funeral. He was well-known in the community and every time someone died, he would be asked to be a pallbearer because Junior had probably been a drinking buddy. Many times when someone died I was the only pastor they knew, as I had lived there all my life. The family would ask me to preach the funeral and Junior would be one of the pallbearers.

After he was saved, as soon as the grave service was over, Junior would come and ask, "Do you think these people understand enough of the Gospel now, that if they go back to plowing and the tractor upsets on them, will they know how to pray to receive Jesus Christ? Or do you think if they go back to cutting timber and the tree falls on them will they know how to accept Christ?"

He would remind me that it takes an hour for the ambulance to get to a person if there is an accident. He thought people needed to know how to be saved because they may die before the ambulance made it to the rural area.

Junior felt strongly that he and I should go to the VA hospital and share with Ike the four spiritual laws on how to be saved. Ike hated our church because we voted against selling alcohol in the township. I was the pastor, so it was natural that he didn't like me. When I went to the VA hospital in Altoona, which was quite a distance from where I live, I walked into his room to tell him that I was there to share with him—if he would like me to—how he could go to Heaven when he died.

Tears ran down Ike's cheek. He told me yes, he would like to know how he could be saved. Ike was only out of the hospital a few weeks when he had another sick spell and was taken back to the hospital. When Junior and I heard that Ike was being released from the hospital, we worried that he would go back to his old friends and start drinking again. But the Lord had another plan. Ike had not been home long when he became ill again. He returned to the hospital where he eventually passed away.

When I was asked to preach Ike's funeral, I felt inadequate. There was a lot of baggage. I was from the same community. I felt that I was a failure because I had to return from Haiti. I felt like a dropout because I didn't return to the mission field, even though I did a great deal of work for missions, speaking to raise awareness, and raising funds for mission projects.

***

Lord, life is a struggle and it is so easy for me to take my eyes off Jesus. It is so easy for me to get depressed, to doubt, to try rather than trust.

Tonight is Sunday School and the church council meeting, and again I feel the need to be controlled by the Holy Spirit totally in every detail of life. Indeed the power of the Holy Spirit to preach, "Would Jesus tolerate your actions in the church?"

I sense a great need for the power of the Holy Spirit. Oh, to be filled! There is a need for something "more" than just claiming to be saved; being able to obey, to trust God anywhere, for anything. God, could You feed, clothe, and protect my family on the mission field in Venezuela, Bangladesh, or Haiti? Could You use a person like me, who has been a dropout, a failure?

Could You give me the language? Would my family be called as surely as I would? I have been struggling with a great restlessness, similar to the times in the corn field before Haiti, the anguish on the ridge at Meadow Gap beside the fallen pine, before the Walnut Grove charge, the troubled days and decisions over Plainfield before being called to Cherry Grove Church of God.

Oh, Lord what is this restlessness about? Why does everything within me cry out for the need of the personal presence and power of Jesus Christ as Lord? Why did WA ask, "Do you know what I mean; 'Jesus Christ as Lord?'" Why did DA ask, "What would you do in the church, if you could do anything you wanted to do, Lester?" implying if I had the power and presence and freedom of the Holy Spirit.

To trust and be guided by the Holy Spirit and not to be hindered by circumstances or what people will think, is my desire. How do I share with the church that there is something "more" than just "getting by" in the Christian life? How do we learn to trust Jesus Christ for everything?

Oh, the anguish of soul I have had as I pray and seek the Lord to fill me with His power and likeness. Yet, I know it is by faith. Not trying. If only I could trust totally by faith the Lord to be in control. If I could only give Him all of my problems, fears, and worries. I have learned some lessons, one is that it is sin to tell God that someone else can do it as well as I can; rather than admit that if God called me, then He will enable me to do it as well as anyone can. I have always told God to get someone else; they could do it better than I could. This is not faith—or trust.

*So **we are Christ's ambassadors**; God is making his appeal through us. We speak for Christ when we plead, "Come back to God!"* (2 Corinthians 5:20 NLT).

Therefore we also pray always for you that our ***God would count you worthy*** *of this calling, and fulfill all the good pleasure of His goodness and the work of faith with power* (2 Thessalonians 1:11 NKJV).

***

Working under the gaze of my father's critical eye took a toll on my self-perception when I was a youth. The Bible says that our identity in Christ means we are worthy, we are glorified in Him, we are made righteous, and we are His ambassadors.

Sadly, for many, the image of a loving heavenly father can be difficult to reconcile with one's impression of their earthly father. I was always criticized. Even though I was a hard worker on the farm, nothing I ever did was ever good enough for him. There was never a "Well done" or "That was a good job."

When he would be away on construction work in the summer, I had all the farming to do plus milk the cows. Even though I worked from daylight till dark as a kid, and even produced more milk than my father, I was always afraid of being criticized, because that's all that I ever knew.

This sore spot in my relationship with my earthly father became an ideal bullseye for my spiritual enemies throughout my life. Though determined to remain steadfast and persevere as a pastor, within the church there was always a critic who made my life miserable. Even though I knew this sore spot was the cause of my doubts, I seemed to be unable to shake it off.

***

> *Jesus left the temple and was walking away when his disciples came up to him to call his attention to its buildings. "Do you see all these things?" he asked. "Truly I tell you, not one stone here will be left on another; every one will be thrown down."*
>
> *As Jesus was sitting on the Mount of Olives, the disciples came to him privately. "Tell us," they said, "when will this happen, and what will be the sign of your coming and of the end of the age?"*

Jesus answered: "Watch out that no one deceives you. For many will come in my name, claiming, 'I am the Messiah,' and will deceive many. You will hear of wars and rumors of wars, but see to it that you are not alarmed. Such things must happen, but the end is still to come. Nation will rise against nation, and kingdom against kingdom. There will be famines and earthquakes in various places. All these are the beginning of birth pains.

"Then you will be handed over to be persecuted and put to death, and you will be hated by all nations because of me. At that time many will turn away from the faith and will betray and hate each other, and many false prophets will appear and deceive many people. Because of the increase of wickedness, the love of most will grow cold, but ***the one who stands firm to the end will be saved*** (Matthew 24:1-13 NIV).

***

It seems I always had a struggle thinking that I should do more for the Lord and questioning if I was doing the best that I could. At this time there was much conflict in the church. Some individuals were quite contentious and desired to have control in the church, causing conflict with others. The church elders and I did the best we could to resolve the issues, but the people causing trouble had contacted the conference superintendent of the denomination and demanded I be removed as pastor. Understandably concerned with what they were being told, the superintendent traveled to Huntingdon County to investigate the claims.

When he came and met with the church and the elders, he saw there was conflict in the church within two factions having different opinions. The superintendent supported the elders and made the decision that I would continue to be the pastor. In predictable fashion, may of the troublemakers left to find another church, and a pastor they could manipulate. Such is the case with wolves in sheep clothing.

***

Because of all the recent conflict, I was considering a move to another church. It seemed I couldn't please everyone at Cherry Grove, nor did I want to conform to whatever ideals they believed a pastor should exemplify. The Bible was my authority, not humans. Apostle Paul's letters to Timothy and to the church in Corinth, in particular, address the orderly way church is supposed to be done, as well as the qualifications and duties of its leaders and elders.

The book of James has always been a continual source of encouragement and direction. Chapter 5 of James speaks directly about being patient and persevering in times of trial, and being careful not to grumble and complain about one another.

I didn't leave Cherry Grove at that time, however, even though doors were opening for me to go elsewhere. It wasn't in me to bolt on a congregation when the going got tough, even in the face of a church election.

The leader of the opposition didn't want to be voted out of his position. Some people on the other side wanted me to support the school teachers strike. I didn't take sides in regard to the school teachers strike. At that time other churches were contacting me to come and be their pastor. Later I would wonder if the decision to stay was the right decision.

***

The Lord opened so many doors during the week of revival when I spoke at New Grenada Church of God. I'm afraid if the Lord would have called me to another place, I would not have made it. I'm afraid it would have ended like Haiti did. I must preach what God wants even if I am fired. I have to preach God's Word; but I don't have to preach if it means compromising the Word. Do I hang on to preaching out of pride? Would I be ashamed, if I didn't have a place to preach? Oh Lord, don't let me stand in Your way at Cherry Grove Church of God; don't let me hang on when I should go, even if it means job hunting somewhere else.

***

Lord, I am all Yours; use me. But Lord, how I need Your strength and Your love. Lord, quiet my troubled heart; congregational meeting, election, and council meeting. Lord, You have helped me through the resignations, others declining the nominations, and the threats of leaving the church. When people rise up against me, I will trust You, Lord. I have never seen a council so treated, to take it so well and not to react.

Thank You, Lord, for bringing us through this ordeal. I realize now that I have never gotten over the defeat of Haiti; and now it seems I can't stand the pressure here, nor can I stand the thought of moving. I fear failure wherever I go. Lord, deliver me of the sin of not trusting You to lead me wherever You call me. It seems so hard to walk by faith.

I felt like David when he wrote Psalm 51. My devotion to the Lord melted into pleading with God to accept me as I am.

I will take heart if the Lord goes with me. I can go anywhere! Oh Lord, it seems my faith is so small when my whole body strains and reacts to the strain and pressure. Must it be like this? Is it just me? Is there a way to live above problems and pressures? It is a challenge just to think about preaching again on Sunday. There is a strong temptation to resign. To give up, to just quit. Oh God, lead me aright. And I thank You for it.

It was a very unsettling time and threatening to me as the pastor. I was never quite sure what another day would bring, or what might happen. There was something new about every day happening in the church. Although the process was difficult, even heartrending at times, I saw Cherry Grove through to the light at the end of the tunnel.

I had no training in conflict resolution. I didn't even believe there should be conflict and confusion in the church. I thought everyone was honest, loving, kind, and cooperative if they were followers of Christ. It was a shock to me that there were nasty and mean people. I had gone through some of the same issues in Haiti—and hoped it would not happen again.

I praise God that the efforts at Cherry Grove would pave the way to a healthier church in the long run. I was eventually vindicated, but not before experiencing the ultimate betrayal that a pastor could get. God delivered me from all the hate and opposition. With the miscreants gone, the health of the church improved and flourished.

***

It is often said when God leads us to do something, we have "a peace about it." This is sometimes called "the peace test," and is assumed to be a confirmation of the Lord's direction. But what about the men in Scripture like Gideon, Moses, and Jeremiah. They didn't feel so peaceful when they were called. In fact they attempted to reason and argue with God, telling Him that He had the wrong person. Virtually every saint in Scripture displayed a form of fear at some time in their lives, even though they were following the Lord.

Even Christ sweat drops of blood; a proven medical phenomena that occurs when someone is under tremendous strain and stress. In the garden of Gethsemane just before His arrest, while deep in prayer and knowing what was about to come, the terror of going to the Cross was almost too much for Him. Though God in the flesh, Jesus was fully human—experiencing the same thoughts, fears, and temptations as the rest of humanity, as the rest of us. He too asked of God if there be another way, while faithfully adding, *"...nevertheless, not My will, but Yours, be done"* (Luke 22:42 NKJV).

I believe there can be both fear and faith. In the midst of awful fear, God can give us faith to face fear. I believe God calls us to certain situations that cause a great deal of anxiety and fear. What about Queen Esther going before the king? I would imagine that she was afraid, but she was called of God to do the right thing even in the midst of fear (see the book of Esther, especially chapter 2).

I have faced a lot of fear in my life but at the same time felt that God was leading me in the situation. Sometimes I had confidence that God was leading me, but I had no illusion that it was going to be easy to face what I felt God was calling me to face. I have a little different view of the "peace test." I believe we can know that we are called of God, and have peace that God is calling us when three things fall in line. One: when God calls, He opens the door. Second: when God calls, He provides the resources. And third: when God calls us to a ministry, He will supply the workers to get the job done.

****

10
How Do You Know?

I had asked a friend, "How do you know when it's time to think about moving?"

His answer, "Pray about it, and if you receive a call to another church, consider it."

As Divine Providence would have it, a call came for a pastor at the New Providence Church of God in Quarryville, Pennsylvania. Quarryville is a small borough in Lancaster County, but the New Providence church had been there about one hundred years. Now they were looking for a new pastor.

I thought back to a few years earlier when working away from home and living in a motel room; and how I had prayed and sought the Lord desperately for direction, for a door to open, and how terrified I was when contacted about pastoring the five churches in the Walnut Grove charge.

Now, over six years later with my academic studies toward a certification of ordination all but complete, I was no less overwhelmed with anxiety about making another move to another church. I was unable to decide on my own without clear direction from the Lord.

I often reflected on Ephesians chapter 6, which encourages believers to be strong in the Lord, and standing firm in His mighty power, and to put on spiritual armor every day, and pray in the Spirit in every circumstance. Without the promises of God as my foundation, I knew I couldn't stand on my own, let alone committing the mission God had called me to do.

***

Sometimes I took time to think about my ancestry. What made me the way that I am. How do you know what influences will make the greatest impression on your life?

The person who influenced me more than any other was my grandpap, Carl Park, born February 21, 1894. I first remember him taking me along to haul in corn with horses and a wagon in 1943 when I was a young lad of 4 years old.

As mentioned previously, in January 1946, I left home in Pittsburgh, at 316 West Street, Wilkinsburg, to go live with my grandparents. I lived with them until 1951.

Grandpap, as I called him, had the faith and courage at the age of 52 years to purchase his own farm located in Maddensville, Pennsylvania—300 acres, with 100 acres tillable. I can't remember a day that was too hot or too long for him to work in the field, or a day that was too cold for him to do the chores. He always saw the sun come up, it was his habit to get up at 5:30 a.m. every day, and wait on God to bring the sun up.

My most memorable time was at night just before bedtime when we would walk and talk as we went to check on the cattle. There were two barns and many times we ended up going to the upper barn on the hill above Maddensville; we never drove or rode, we always walked.

Two incidents I remember the most was when a cow's head was stuck between the boards in the barn, and a heifer that was butted into the water trough. We always got them out of their predicaments. Grandpap and I would always check on sick animals and those due to deliver a calf.

He taught me to work, save, and invest. When I was 6 years old, he told me to save enough to buy a calf. I used Kodak film containers to save my nickels in. My first calf cost $15.00 and I was in business for the rest of my life. Grandpap gave me $7.50 back, his half, as he and Uncle Wayne were in partnership.

There was nothing in this world that I would rather do than work with Grandpap, it was never a chore or burden working with him. He was always a source of encouragement; when the day was done, he would always compliment and support me for the amount of work we had accomplished.

Grandpap was that way with me until he died in May 1966, he never complained about hard times, hard work, or not having a fair break in life. He taught me to buy cattle, telling me they would grow in value; and he encouraged me to buy the Giles Farm two years before he died. It turned out to be a great investment.

He taught me that there is only one standard—God's standard. I remember we threw down enough loose hay on a Saturday to feed the livestock on Sunday, as his faith led him to attend church, not when it was convenient but whenever there was a church service.

I learned what to preach from my grandparents and how to preach from the evangelist and preachers they took me to hear, wherever a church was having revival meetings. I sat with my grandfather in Sunday school until I was a teenager. During those years the preachers were invited to our house for dinner, they were respected and honored.

When I was 15 years old, Grandpap confronted me with the need to commit my life to obeying Jesus. When I went to revival a spring night in 1955, I was ready to go to the altar and turn my life over to Christ when Reverend Boyle gave the invitation.

Most of everything that has happened to me was due to the influence of my grandparents, including the calling to be a missionary, pastor, evangelist, and church planter.

My grandmother, Fannie Lane Park, born April 19, 1896, was the seventh child of 14 children raised by her parents, Dutton and Elizabeth Lane. She was a stern lady, a manager, and able to save and survive. It was no problem for her to cook a groundhog or eat suckers (fish) we got from the creek. Anything we drug in, she cleaned and cooked.

Grandma's influence spanned a century. She was 50 when she started raising me and she didn't seem old to me. She planted a huge garden, canned, butchered, heated water in an iron kettle over a wood fire to wash clothes, and made lye soap out of leftover fat. I remember her cooking on a wood stove, and the time when she bought her first refrigerator. Before that, she kept things cold in water at the pump house. She never wasted anything; our clothes were patched until they ended up as braided rugs on the floor.

Grandma taught me to visit the sick; she would take me along with her to visit people who were dying at home. If they breathed hard with a rattle or gurgle in their throat, she said that was a "death rattle" and the person would not live much longer. She visited people no matter who they were.

She taught me great respect for the things of God and encouraged me every step of the way in becoming a missionary and a pastor. At age 80, she attended my ordination service.

I am often reminded of my heritage; often I have wondered how Dutton and Elizabeth Lane raised 14 children on the Brad Rogers Farm at Meadow Gap in Pennsylvania. Dutton could sew up a cow or horse, build a house, and run a store—all without government help or social security.

It was and is good for children to grow up having to work and make a good life for their family. Dutton ran the general store in Meadow Gap, then in the later years moved to Pogue and built a house and store there. I remember Grandma Lane living there when Mom and Dad ran the store at Pogue from 1946-1950.

Grandma Lane died during this time; she was from the Fernburg family, born in Maddensville. Dutton and Elizabeth left a few dollars and property when they died. Grandpap Lane was a descendant of Samuel Lane who was a preacher and church planter in Huntington County before 1800, planting Old School Baptist churches.

Many of the Lanes visited our home often. Most were confident and competent people who made their mark in the world. I witnessed to some of them; however they were taught predestination and election and believed they were predestined to salvation or damnation and there was nothing they could do to accept or reject Jesus. They didn't understand the sovereignty of God and personal responsibility. I baptized Aunt Mertie in a creek at Maddensville; she was a sister of Grandma's.

I often think of my great grandparents, Clay and Alice Park, Grandpap Carl's parents. Alice's maiden name was Hudson, a small lady who raised a large family and attended the Baptist church. Clay was a pleasant man, with a bushy mustache as I remember him. He owned the land from Three Springs to Saltillo and up to the Three Springs Farms area. He traveled by train to work in Huntingdon at the County Conservation Office and was also on the draft board. Clay also ran a store in Three

Springs, selling farm machinery and fertilizer. During that time, Grandpap Carl farmed for him.

Grandpap Carl told me about delivering farm machinery and setting it up, driving the team of horses that pulled the hearse, hauling coal with a team from the mine at Joller, grading the road and pulling a dump wagon with a team of horses when the road to Maddensville was built—all while he was also farming at the same time.

***

Yes, I learned a lot from my grandparents, for which I am eternally grateful. God was watching over me as a child and continued throughout my life. For example, when at a loss for ideas for a sermon message, I would pray—and every time, God delivered.

I still remember thinking that if God gave me one sermon I would be good for the first two weeks. I could use the same sermon in all five churches. Each church had worship every two weeks. I don't know if I ever gave any thought as to what I was going to do for the next fifty weeks. I know if it is God's will, He will open the doors, provide the resources, and supply all our needs.

A move to a new church meant possibly leaving behind some unresolved issues, as well as the process of getting acquainted with an entirely new group of people, with an entirely new set of issues, in an entirely new place. At least Quarryville was in a lovely rural area in the heart of Amish farm country.

I dreaded the city because I was very shy. People frightened me. Being in front of people and speaking in front of a group terrified me. I was a country boy and had no interest in the cities since I left home in Wilkinsburg, Pennsylvania, in second grade, and moved to the country.

Dolores and I eventually agreed to take the call to New Providence Church. That spring, I finished the last of 61 ministerial training courses, and became a certified minister. I didn't think I would ever get all the work finished, and take all the exams.

But with God's help, I did.

How did we know we made the right decision? We didn’t, but God did.

****

11
Prepare My Heart, Lord

My January 1977 prayer to the good Lord went something like this:

I thank You, Lord, for Your goodness. I believe my anxiety, depression, and anger is because of my childhood experiences; of thinking that I could never do anything good enough for my dad. But now I can never be good enough to please *me.* The real problem is that I am my own parent.

Lord, help me not to criticize myself or depreciate myself. I have feared someone will be critical of me, and find my work unsatisfactory. That person is me. If everyone else thinks my work is ok, I still feel it's not good enough. Oh Lord, what irrational fear! Please deliver me from my own criticism. Help me, Lord, to accept myself, my work, and my sermons.

If You accept me, then Lord, help me accept myself. If I am all right, then give me peace. If I'm doing all right from Your point of view, then give me the satisfaction to know that. If I'm not doing all right, if my life or work is not good enough, then Lord, please show me what I need to be doing and I will do it.

Lord, help me to be a loving parent to myself. Thank You, Lord. I think I am my own critical parent. I treat myself like I am used to being treated. May this year be filled with Your lovingkindness and mercy and grace. In Jesus' precious and holy name, amen.

***

In April 1977 I wrote that it was a beautiful day; all my needs were met, the taxes were paid, the freezer was full, there were six steers in the pasture, money in the bank, the family is healthy, my wife is loving and kind, the salary is sufficient, the church is doing good, and my work has been complimented. Hallelujah!

Yet, I wonder why more people are not being saved. Then when I read about Christ, I see He never ran after people, but He did offer them eternal life. Why do I feel I must run men down and force Christ upon them? Lord, deliver me I pray. You have led me all the way. You led me into the ministry, and surely Your power is sufficient for this work.

Lord, have your way in this church; prepare hearts for revival, and use me. Forgive me for failing to trust You. Lord, use me to witness to whoever they may be and wherever I may meet them. Amen.

***

Grandma Park passed away on May 9, 1977. Jeff and I had visited her on May 6. Although she was paralyzed, she reached up with her good hand and squeezed mine. She couldn't talk, but it seemed evident that she knew we were there. There is hope and assurance in Christ. It is something to live 81 years for the Lord. She had her ways; but one thing I must say, she never wavered in her faith in Christ. She made her mark on me. Oh, the godly influence Grandma and Grandpap had on many people—on me especially.

My grandparents were the dearest people on earth to me. They attended revival or evangelistic services in all the neighboring churches for miles around. I think that that is where I learned to preach, because I heard many of the visiting evangelists.

I remember that whatever Grandpap and I brought in from the creek or the woods or the field, Grandma would "do it up," and we would eat it. She heated water in an iron kettle over a fire outside, and carried it into the wash house to wash our clothes. She would patch our clothes for as long as they would hold a patch. And when they could not be patched anymore, she would tear them into strips of rags and weave rugs out of them for the floor. She raised and canned almost all of our food. I remember her saving fat and lard, then putting it in a big kettle with banner lye to make laundry soap.

My grandparents were both hardworking and frugal people. My grandfather was 52 years old when he bought the farm, and started farming for himself. There was no day that was too hot or too long for him to work. My fondest memories are tagging along with him as a little kid all day long. It was my job to feed the calves; that's how I started in the cattle business. Always at night, before we went to bed, we would take a flashlight and go out to check on all the cattle.

My grandparents always raised a large garden, and preserved and canned enough food for us to make it through the winter. My grandmother weeded the garden, and I would haul the weeds out to feed the pigs. I picked black walnuts in the fall of the year and brought them to the house in my wagon. When the walnuts dried, my grandmother would crack them out of the shell and use them to make cookies and cakes. I still have a fondness to this day for black walnut trees. I planted a few but was never very successful.

Before my grandparents bought their first electric refrigerator, we would put food in a mason jar and take it to the springhouse, putting it in the cold ground water to keep from spoiling until we ate it. My grandmother cooked on a wood stove for a long time until she purchased a gas range to cook on. Life was sure not easy, but it sure was good living with them as a child.

We played board games with Grandma, and then before bedtime we had a Bible reading. The Bible was of utmost importance to my grandparents. For them it was not something to know about, or believe about, it was something to put into practice in everyday life. My grandparents were not into arguing about Scriptures. They were into obeying God's Word.

Often my grandmother invited the pastor or the guest preacher to our house for dinner. My grandmother visited people who were sick and dying, and at that time it was at home. She impressed upon me the importance of visiting the sick and dying.

Think love, not hate.
Think success, not failure.
Think health, not disease.
Think good, not evil.
Think prosperity, not poverty.
Think safety, not danger.
Think life, not death.
Think friendship, not hostility.
Think joy, not sorrow.
Think hope, not despair.
Think tranquility, not tension.
Look forward, not backward.

These are personal guidelines of John Harris, now in his second century.

***

There was less tension and bickering at the new church in Quarryville. The people of New Providence Church of God were more respectful and affirming of my leadership and open to accepting and trying new ideas. There were the usual battles with sin and general apathy to the Word of God. How could anyone be apathetic to the saving power of Christ? The thirsting souls in Haiti would never take the grace of God for granted. It never ceased to amaze me how comparatively dull the hearts of most Western Christians were. But as always, I chose to trust God, not my fickle emotions.

We need to be far more committed to Christ than just being concerned about church repairs and people attending. We need to be committed to sharing the Gospel with people in a way that their lives will be transformed.

By June, it was obvious that Jeff was unhappy since moving to the Quarryville area. This was as issue that bothered Dolores especially, as she didn't like seeing her firstborn son feeling downtrodden and frustrated. Jeff was having a difficult time adjusting, being 15 years old. He had left his friends and his good job behind. Probably a lot of it was my fault because I was too busy to give the boys much time and attention.

As autumn changed to winter, and the year drew to a close, I was ever so grateful for my wife, Dolores, who had stuck with me through everything. I compared God's love for me with my love for Dolores. She was very supportive of me in the ministry and when we went to Haiti in 1967. I learned through our marriage how God's grace and goodness covers all of our shortcomings. It is interesting how when one admits that life is a struggle, it gets a little easier; and when we admit we are powerless to accomplish anything ourselves, it empowers us.

***

My 1977 end-of-year prayer:

Dear Lord help me to live for Jesus, not men.
Help me to glorify Jesus. Not Lester.
Help me to let Jesus measure my work,
rather than concerning myself with how I measure up to men's standards.
Help me to please Jesus, not others.
Lord help me to be honest with myself and with You.
Why must I feel guilty when I sit down, take a day off, or go hunting?
Lord, I desire to see the church become real in living, in loving, and in concern.
Help us to be honest with one another,
rather than fake it that we never have any problems or temptations.
Lord, guide us in the New Year, help me to venture;
to follow Your will, wherever it leads.

***

My wonderings at the end of the year:

- Is it a waste of time to build churches?
- Is it a waste of money, God's money, to pay pastors?
- Is it God's way?
- Is it right to fuss about Sunday school rooms, painting the church, paving the parking lot, paying the pastor, when lost and dying people are falling into hell?
- Oh God, where are we when people die without Christ?
- When we have a four-hour board meeting, and only see eleven people saved in 1977. Oh God, where are we going?
- What will happen to the church?
- Oh, Lord, what would You have me to do? To be?
- Help me never be satisfied with lukewarm commitments to my Christ.
- Lord kindle a fire in me that will never let me sit down and fold my hands and let the world go to hell.
- *"For God did not send his Son into the world to condemn the world, but to save the world through him"* (John 3:17).
- Lord turn me on for You; live Your life through me.
- How can the church be a church "honoring Christ," not a building or organization?

- Should we believers be the church, and do the work of Christ? Could we do it better without buildings and full-time preachers?

***

In the States, 1977 was a relatively uneventful year. Jimmy Carter was sworn in as the 39th United States President. The first personal home computer, the Commodore PET, was unveiled to the public. The science-fiction film *Star Wars* debuted in theaters, New York City experienced a 25-hour blackout, and Elvis Presley passed away in his Graceland home at age 42. About 75,000 fans filled the streets of Memphis for his funeral.

The year came and went in Haiti much as it had for many years—the impoverished living off the land and on what little employment they could find in the city, while the elite few lived in ridiculous extravagance.

I had continued to travel with work groups to Haiti during the year and took any opportunity to do missions work there, or elsewhere. I finally felt I was making a real difference for the Kingdom of God. As hard as the work could be, it was a joy to do. Truly God had prepared my heart.

****

12
God's Will Be Done

In 1978 I was beginning to wonder what the future held, especially now that I was back to doing a bit of farming again, renting from my dad to work on his farm. I enjoyed farming, and did it to the best of my ability. I was giving careful consideration to the idea of working full-time for Dad once again. Such an option seemed more appealing than ministry, at this point. From my father's property, I could look across the creek and see the farm I sold before going to Haiti in 1967. I always felt "at home" on a farm.

I would often recite a Haitian saying, "Si se volonte Bondye," which means "If it is God's will." So many things about Haiti had influenced me, and yet it was because of my experience as a farmer that I initially moved to Haiti, expecting to continue farming there. To quit farming altogether was never part of the plan.

After I had been back home a few years, Dad's health failed and he was not able to farm anymore. So he asked me if I wanted to farm the home place. It was a small farm and the boys and I generally did the farming on Saturdays or during my annual week of vacation.

I eventually purchase the farm from my parents. When our sons were no longer available to help with the work, I rented the land to a farmer. I never went back to full-time farming; I simply couldn't bear turning my back on what I knew to be God's calling.

In June 1978, I picked up a magazine and read an article about missionaries. I just felt I had to go to prayer and commit my life to Christ for whatever use He has for it. While I was praying, Dolores brought the mail in. There was a letter from the Secretary of Missions for the Churches of God stating the need for a "leader for project help…Haiti."

I was touched by this request. It was a matter of prayer and fasting. So many questions flooded my mind. Lord, am I the man for the job? Would Dolores be willing to go again? How can I ever get the courage to ask her? What about the boys? We seem to have so many challenges with them. What about leaving Jeff behind? What about the farm? What about their schooling in Haiti?

The first time we went to Haiti it was a step into the unknown. Now I know many of the heartaches, tears, sorrows, and problems. Lord, it will take more faith than I have now to tackle all these problems. I'll soon be 40 years old and I have always been afraid. But Lord, I'm more afraid to be out of Your will. I still feel the call to missions. Lord, I need a clear call or sign from You that I am Your man for this job. Is it just my own mind, my own ego seeking the glory of being a missionary? Am I deceived into thinking it would be easy?

I know how hard it is to give up, to give in and go, to give up everything, to say goodbye. Lord, I have it better here and now than ever before. I've never had it so good, and never been treated so well. I'd bawl if I had to leave these people. My new salary is twelve thousand dollars starting July 1, 1978.

So many things need to be done here, and in the conference. It was suggested that I should serve on Missions and Church Development, which was responsible for church planting. I was already promoting church planting in the denomination, and was currently planting the High View Church of God at Strasburg, Pennsylvania, at around that time. It seemed a good fit.

I asked Dolores to consider the request to return to Haiti and pray about it. However, Dolores was not at all interested in returning once again to Haiti to live; not after settling into life in Pennsylvania for the past decade. We had just recently moved to a new church and parsonage. The children were older and in greater number, and the eldest ones had individual lives and responsibilities of their own. For Dolores, the answer was no. She had given Haiti a chance, twice, and was unwilling to discuss the matter further, let alone try a third time.

I still believed God not only called me to Haiti in 1967, but He also gave me a burden in my heart for Haiti that has never lifted.

***

Lord, I have a hundred more excuses why I should not go to Haiti again. And I know that if You can solve one, You can solve a hundred. I don't know anyone else who wants to go, who has experience in Haiti, knows some of the language, has the interest and experience in church growth and development, and training in teaching witnessing to others.

It has been in my heart, my prayers, my dreams, and my vision, no matter where I am or what I am doing for over the past eleven long years—it has been my vision all these years to see the church of Jesus Christ established in Haiti and many Haitians won to Jesus.

After prayer, I turned to Colossians 1:9-12 (NKJV):

> *For this reason we also, since the day we heard it, do not cease to pray for you, and to ask that you may be filled with the knowledge of His will in all wisdom and spiritual understanding; that you may walk worthy of the Lord, fully pleasing Him, being fruitful in every good work and increasing in the knowledge of God; strengthened with all might, according to His glorious power, for all patience and longsuffering with joy; giving thanks to the Father who has qualified us to be partakers of the inheritance of the saints in the light.*

I prayed over and over that we would be filled with His mighty glorious strength so to keep going no matter what happens…always full of the joy of the Lord. Amen.

Dear Lord, if You want me to go to Haiti, make it clear. Where is the Samuel who makes the call clear? (See 1 Samuel 3:1-8 NKJV.)

***

The people are very cooperative at this church, but they seem to be without a burden for lost souls, or too reserved to share it. There seems to be a drought here of spiritual interest. Lord, may I be open and tuned to Your direction for these kind people. There had been a drought of spiritual interest in the church. The people are much warmer than any of the churches I had served. It seems like an ideal arrangement. I have never pastored a group of people who are more loving, kind, and supportive of their pastor.

The New Providence Church of God was also very supportive of world missions and church planting—very generous in giving to the needs brought to their attention. They are a very good group of people to work with.

However, I was concerned by their lack of desire for spiritual growth, and for the lost souls in the community. I tried hard to get people involved in discipleship and evangelism. I guess I thought everyone should be as excited about discipleship, and evangelism and church planting and missions as I was. Those were my goals. And I was very passionate for those goals.

> *If my people, which are called by my name, shall humble themselves, and pray, and seek my face, and turn from their wicked ways; then will I hear from heaven, and will forgive their sin, and will heal their land* (2 Chronicles 7:14).

***

In January 1979, we decided to stay in Pennsylvania. Preaching became easier and winning men and women to Christ burns in my bones, church growth/church planting is on my mind. Personal evangelism is my burden. Haiti is still a burden; and my cry is still, "Help me, Lord, today, to experience peace and know Your will!"

I started off the New Year by writing down all the things I want to do for God in my lifetime:

- Win souls.
- Be part of church planting in Haiti and the U.S.
- Lead the Churches of God in training people in personal evangelism, church growth principles, and church planting.
- See the ministerial course opened to all people called to minister.
- Lead my entire family to Christ and challenge all my sons to be part of world evangelism.
- Challenge people to enter the ministry
- Reach the unsaved and provide a fellowship where they can be discipled.
- See a church established for my friends in Maddensville.
- See Highview Church of God go for God.
- See New Providence Church have revival, reach the community, and mother new churches.

- Train soul winners.
- Look for God's way to reproduce reproducers.

Only one life, 'twill soon be past,
Only what's done for Christ will last.
I want God's will for my life…
Nothing more,
Nothing less,
Nothing else.
(From Grandma Park's plaque on her wall.)

Lord, I pray to see a fellowship loving and reaching out into the world. I want to be like Christ in concern for people. I have seen God answer prayers regarding our sons. Lord, You have been so good; help me to equip the members here, and to encourage church planting here and in Haiti. It is Your will that counts, not my accomplishments, so I will not boast (see James 4:16).

Lord, I would like to use my life in world evangelization. I believe we should be planting many indigenous churches in Haiti; I want to be part of it, if You will, Lord. I want to see lay people here in the U.S. equipped for the ministry and for missionary work.

"Whatever we ask we receive from Him, because we keep His commandments and do those things that are pleasing in His sight" (1 John 3:22) If we do God's will and keep His commandments, whatever we ask we receive. Oh, to do God's will and to keep His commandments!

***

At the end of 1979, I can see a vast possibility here at this church, but we lack faith. We have not continued to expand the number of Sunday school classes. There is a lack of interest in revival and no concern to reach the lost. There is negative attitude; not a positive attitude of faith.

I pray that God will soon tell me what to do about the church; it seems the whole burden is on my back. Lord, is it that I have not depended on You? Is it that I have done things my way? And not sought or waited on You, Lord? Lord, what do I do? I seek Your perfect will.

Newly established Highview Church seems to be going well; three weeks of revival services are scheduled. Also, I am to speak to the Harrisburg ministerium. I pray that the Lord will lead me to speak what He wants me to say.

***

I believe that the higher level of faith we have, the more positive rather than negative we are. When we lack faith we tend to be good at coming up with excuses. For example, we make the excuse that people are not interested in Christ, or they aren't interested in attending church—so we don't make the effort to reach out to people.

Another example is if we lack faith we tend to say things like, "Oh why plant another new church? There are plenty of existing churches and plenty of room for people if they really want to attend church." Lack of faith does not see the potential of what can happen when we plant a new church, when we disciple a new Christian, when we start a program like Celebrate Recovery. Lack of faith is an excuse for laziness. But God will make a way.

I tend to put the blame on myself when things don't move forward. Yet I know that everybody in the church has a mind and a will—and they can make choices to support programs or not to support programs. The pastor can have ideas and make suggestions, but a pastor has no power to make people do the things he is passionate about. I am finally learning this hard lesson.

Certainly on a very positive a note for 1979, our sons Kirby and Kevin officially gave their lives to the Lord! And I spent quality time hunting and fishing with our sons. The Lord's will was done in our lives too many times to count—His faithfulness remains true and steady.

****

13
Destiny

Two months into the new decade, and a near brush with tragedy occurred when our eldest son, Jeff, was attempting to pass another vehicle and his automobile rolled several times after veering into a ditch and through a field. The accident occurred on a Sunday afternoon, when I was about to begin preaching a week of revival services that evening. The vehicle was totaled. Miraculously, Jeff and his friend who was riding in the front passenger seat, walked away from the wreck. I asked Jeff, "Did you have time to get right with the Lord?" He said he was too busy holding on to the steering wheel as the car rolled over and over. We all thanked God for His mercy and protection.

I continued to go to Haiti as often as possible with a work team or for a speaking event, but it wasn't often enough. From the moment I landed until the moment I departed for the airport, I had to remain focused on the task at hand.

I regularly prayed about my destiny in Haiti, if there was one. I couldn't uproot our family against their will or abandon them to go live in the most impoverished nation in the Western hemisphere. I wondered, *Do I need to go to the same extent the apostles did when they abandoned their families and their business, without hesitation, to follow Jesus? Does doing anything less mean I'm not a true Christian?* These questions are much more common among Christians than some may think, and perhaps this is the very conversation the church needs to have.

In July 1980, my name was submitted for the position of Associate in Ministry at the general conference level under the head of the denomination. Other people had far more confidence in me than I had in myself. I was reluctant to even consider the offer.

***

Time goes by so fast; I feel I never get enough done. Being a pastor of a church, preaching, and being a parent is a lot to do well. I wish I could do better. Lord, help me list my priorities. There is such a need in this world; youth, marriages, preaching, counseling, church-planting, evangelism, encouraging people into full-time Christian service, and missions.

Lord, show me Your will for my life is a constant prayer.

An article in the July-August issue of the *Signal:* "Opportunities in Haiti seem to be almost unlimited, but we are woefully short on American leadership. There is a need for a registered nurse, pharmacist, and permanent director."

I struggle with where I should be. It's hard to decide. I feel I do an all right job as pastor, but I continue to struggle with the call to Haiti. Is it because of the need that has existed all these years? Could I deal with the heat, the responsibilities, the boys' schooling, and all that is involved? Why must I always be challenged and burdened for the Lord's work that is beyond my feeling of being qualified?

The Lord reminds me to look at my strengths or gifts that He gave me. Would I rather lay my head on the pillow for the last time knowing I had tried and failed, or knowing I had never tried? What would have happened in Haiti, if I had never tried? What would have happened at Walnut Grove, if I had never tried; at New Providence Church of God or at Highview Church of God, if I had never tried? Every time the Lord has called, I knew I couldn't. But the Lord knew I could!

Lord, how much faith does it take? How do I know Your will, my destiny? I want to do the right thing and I don't want to live with regret. I want to look back at the end of my life and say honestly, "Jesus led me all the way."

Lord, I don't know if I am willing. But I would like to be.

***

> *Even the righteousness of God, through faith in Jesus Christ, to all and on all who believe. For there is no difference* (Romans 3:22 NKJV).

I agree that God is strong in my weakness. I know for a fact that everything that God called me to do—being a missionary to Haiti, a pastor, a church planter—I was not humanly qualified to do. God gave me the strength to do what He called me to do.

I had to decide if God was calling me to stay where I was, while at the same time being called to go to another place? I thought about, *What is God's will in the bigger picture and how does God's will work in regard to what is good for my children? If it looks like a good opportunity for me, but it's not going to be healthy for my children, I need to reconsider. Just because it's a higher position, with more prestige, power, or pay does not mean that it is God's will, or that it is best for my family.*

First Corinthians chapter 10 reveals three ways to make a decision:

1. Is it going to bring glory to God?
2. Is it for the good of others?
3. Will it promote the growth of the church?

The Scripture passage says at the end of the chapter, *"that many may be saved."* I encourage you to read chapter 10 in 1 Corinthians. There is wisdom for the ages contained in every verse.

There's a very great need in this world for authentic preaching and for transparent preachers who live out what they preach. The need is also greater every day for good parenting, in a troubled world. Sound marriage teaching, is needed as much now as ever.

***

> *Then the Pharisees and scribes asked Him* [Jesus], *"Why do Your disciples not walk according to the tradition of the elders, but eat bread with unwashed hands?" He answered and said to them, "Well did Isaiah prophesy of you hypocrites, as it is written: 'This people honors Me with their lips, but their heart is far from Me. And in vain they worship Me, Teaching as doctrines the commandments of men.' For laying aside the commandment of God, you hold the tradition of men—the washing of pitchers and cups, and many other such things you do." He said to them,* ***"All too well you reject the commandment of God, that you may keep your tradition"*** (Mark 7:5-9 NKJV).

One day, while Jesus and His disciples were dining and communing with some lost souls, the religious hypocrites of the day demanded to know why He and His disciples did not follow the religious tradition of ritual handwashing. Christ often shook the religious leaders of the day, not just by exposing their true character, but by challenging their traditions and assumptions.

If being a Christian means to emulate Christ, then perhaps that means there are times when Christians need to shake things up too; to challenge traditions, speak up for truth, and even risk offending someone to the point that they may want to crucify you.

This truth is clearly laid out in Scripture. God's will is clear; yet some Christians are unwilling to witness, visit those who are ill, start new programs to help meet needs in the community such as marriage counseling, preparing for parenthood, Christian living, understanding God's calling in one's life, and recovery programs for people in need of healing.

The stubbornness and shortsightedness of some Christians was inexcusable. The modern American Christian was becoming irrelevant and impotent. Church attendance dwindled in the 1970s, and the '80s weren't looking any better. In Western culture, a new wave of decadence and excess was bombarding American Christians with more distractions than ever.

I never paid much attention to television so it was hard for me to imagine how music videos, late-night sketch comedy shows, video games, and profanity and violence in prime time television and news were desensitizing the U.S., and taking a visible toll on the church.

New Providence Church of God is located in Providence Township, in Lancaster County Pennsylvania. The township grew by 68 percent in the 1970s. Area churches did not grow by that same percentage. Most churches were not growing at all in the '70s. This deeply bothered me. Everywhere I looked, I saw great opportunity for church growth, but few people shared my enthusiasm and work ethic.

I was not completely on my own, however. I was blessed to have a handful of likeminded parishioners in my corner. One in particular was

Joe, a leader in the Church of God who also saw opportunities for growth. He believed in the concept of elective classes, giving people options and opportunities for classes or small groups. I appreciated Joe's ideas and did my best to implement them wherever possible.

But change was scary for most church-goers who had never seen church done this way. They'd say, "We've always done it this way, and it was good enough in the past, so why change now?" Change is not quick nor easy. It is more showing than telling. But there is a stubborn belief that *tradition* is most important.

***

January 1, 1981

The New Year brought with it many questions regarding my destiny at New Providence Church, including: Lord, do You really care where I serve? Does it matter to You whether I stay here or leave? What would be best for my boys? For Dolores? Does it matter to You whether I go to Haiti or not? Or to Findlay, Ohio, for the General Conference of the Churches of God staff position? How do I know if I am the person You want for either of these jobs?

> *And whoever does not carry their cross and follow me cannot be my disciple. Suppose one of you wants to build a tower. Won't you first sit down and estimate the cost to see if you have enough money to complete it? For if you lay the foundation and are not able to finish it, everyone who sees it will ridicule you, saying, "This person began to build and wasn't able to finish"* (Luke 14:27-30 NIV).

***

For every question, God had the answer.

It finally was sinking in that I could preach or lead, but it's up to the people whether they want to respond or get involved. It is very easy to be a leader when people want to follow. Just as it's very easy to raise good children if they desire to obey and do the right thing. But it's pretty hard to raise a prodigal. That was my dilemma at times.

I could not deny feeling forever connected to that small island nation with so much hope, joy, potential, and beauty, in spite of the harsh living conditions. But my visits became fewer and farther between as the 1980s progressed toward chaos in Haiti.

***

I was preaching twice on Sundays, often teaching Sunday school as well, leading Bible study on Wednesday evenings, as well as speaking at conference events in the denomination, and any other place requested—so I could talk about the need in Haiti. I continued working on church planting and served as chairman on the Commission of Missions and Church Development, the commission responsible for planting new churches and working to restore failing ones.

I was a compulsive workaholic. I worked on holidays and I used a couple of weeks of my vacation time to work on the farm. The family and I would go Friday evening to the farm and work on Saturdays, and then return to the New Providence Church for Sunday services.

Although the Bible strongly recommends taking a break from our labors once a week, I believed working hard and working well was the solution to living wholeheartedly for the Lord. But doing this perfectly, I knew was impossible. There is both the sovereignty of Almighty God, and human responsibility. One without the other is false teaching.

Yes, God is sovereign; while at the same time, the other side of the coin, is human responsibility and accountability. We can't hide behind the sovereignty of God. If we do, we come up with false beliefs such as: I don't believe in evangelism or missions, because that's the sovereign work of God.

No. That completely ignores the Great Commission, which says in Matthew 28:16-20 (NLT):

> *Then the eleven disciples left for Galilee, going to the mountain where Jesus had told them to go. When they saw him, they worshiped him—but some of them doubted!*

Jesus came and told his disciples, "I have been given all authority in heaven and on earth. Therefore, go and make disciples of all the nations, baptizing them in the name of the Father and the Son and the Holy Spirit. Teach these new disciples to obey all the commands I have given you. And be sure of this: I am with you always, even to the end of the age."

****

14
The People Are His Servants

*Therefore I tell you, **do not worry about your life**, what you will eat or drink; or about your body, what you will wear. Is not life more than food, and the body more than clothes? Look at the birds of the air; they do not sow or reap or store away in barns, and yet your heavenly Father feeds them. Are you not much more valuable than they? **Can any one of you by worrying add a single hour to your life?** And why do you worry about clothes? See how the flowers of the field grow. They do not labor or spin. Yet I tell you that not even Solomon in all his splendor was dressed like one of these. If that is how God clothes the grass of the field, which is here today and tomorrow is thrown into the fire, will he not much more clothe you—you of little faith? So do not worry, saying, "What shall we eat?" or "What shall we drink?" or "What shall we wear?" For the pagans run after all these things, and your heavenly Father knows that you need them. But **seek first his kingdom and his righteousness, and all these things will be given to you as well. Therefore do not worry about tomorrow, for tomorrow will worry about itself.** Each day has enough trouble of its own* (Matthew 6:25-34 NIV).

What does Jesus mean when He says, *"do not worry about your life, what you will eat"*…and *"do not worry about tomorrow"?* Matthew 6:33 (NKJV) says, *"But seek first the kingdom of God and His righteousness, and all these things shall be added to you."*

He certainly is not telling us not to plan, work, or provide. He is saying the worrying about tomorrow's food, clothes, and needs; the worry, the fear, etc. causes us to lose sleep, develop physical issues, and lose our peace—His peace. We die from these things, not from the lack of necessary provisions to sustain our lives.

God takes care of the birds when they migrate; surely He is not any less faithful to take care of His preachers. He always has and He has never taken care of us better than He has this past year.

The Lord has taught me that I need to cool the worrying and fretting, the anger and bitterness when things don't go well, when people don't agree with me, when they won't serve, when they are not faithful, and when they don't live righteous lives.

The *Lord* is the Head of the Church, not me. The church is Christ's body. They serve Him, not me. They obey Him, they are faithful to Him, not to the denomination or preacher. If I believe in the priesthood of all believers, they are the ones who are responsible for their own lives, and as members and leaders, they are also responsible for their church.

I feel good knowing that Christ is the Head, and the church is His, and the people are His servants. When they don't attend, they are His. When they aren't faithful, they are His. When they won't serve, they are His. When they go astray, they are His.

Another thing God taught me is that He answers prayers, keeps covenants, and will bring to pass (in His time) our desires to fulfill His will. It was not my doings that I was elected to Missions and Church Development as chairman; and elected to Commission on World Missions. All glory goes to God.

By the end of 1983, I was praising the Lord for answering my prayers about planting churches; He opened the door in the towns of Manheim and Greencastle. Also a new church is being planted in Haiti; Lancaster/York Missionary Rally are picking up the tab for the first several years.

My constant prayer these days are, "Lord, break and burden our hearts with a holy desire to do Your will; beginning with me. Help me, Lord, not to be so upset with people who don't want to obey You or do Your will. Lord, lead us to additional places to plant churches in 1984. Lord, I desire to know your will about staying here; I feel led to mission churches. It hurts me to be negative, but I don't see any hope here, short of a revival. Lord, if there is going to be a change here, it will have to be by Your Spirit. Lord, have Your way in my life, the church, and the conference program of church planting."

***

As I studied and prayed I came to understand that the people in the church belong to Jesus, not to Lester Swope. They are the Lord's sheep, not mine. I could only preach the Word. Jesus has to convict the church.

I have pondered much over the years and I have come to the conclusion that perfectionists lie to themselves. They always feel inadequate or insufficient. They can never tell themselves the truth that they have done well, or done enough. I look back over my entire life and I see what I accomplished with God's help. Many people affirmed my work; but I have a different opinion about myself.

I was often worried about the wandering souls in our church, the crucial unmet needs in Haiti and the current devastation taking place there. Family concerns also swarmed through my mind.

I led the Bible study at the Manheim Church of God. A friend of mine led the Bible study at Greencastle. I learned there was a church building for sale in Manheim, and the Commission on Missions and Church Development decided to buy it. We painted it and started holding services there.

***

Telling Yourself the Truth was a book that came highly recommended by a radio pastor. I listened to WDAC radio every Sunday morning before leaving for the church service. The popular book, co-authored by William Backus and Marie Chapian, is a well-regarded counseling and therapy tool in Christian circles, based upon biblical methods of beating depression, anxiety, fear, anger, and other common problems. The authors are responsible for coining the term "Misbelief Therapy." I found the resource very useful in overcoming fears and doubts. However, saying positive things about myself, *to myself,* was a radically foreign concept; one that took time to adjust to.

I learned from the book that you can lie to yourself. You can be influenced as a child to feel that you don't measure up, that you're of no account, and/or that you can't do anything right. It was really a challenge for me to start telling myself the truth. The book was an eye-opener for me.

The authors suggest readers write in a notebook what to tell myself about *me,* every day. I wrote:

> I am well off, I have it made, and I have a good family. I have a good job, I am well-treated and loved. I have a nice place to live. I am appreciated for my hard work and caring for people. I am getting things accomplished in World Missions and planting churches at home.
>
> This past week, Missions and Church Development Commission of the Churches of God purchased a church building at Manheim, Pa. We have home Bible studies there and at Greencastle, Pa. We are working on, and praying for Bible studies at Chambersburg and Hummelstown, Pa.
>
> I need to realize how much I am getting accomplished, and to feel good about it; rather than feeling I don't get enough done, or don't do things well enough.

I often struggle with the thought that I'm not a good enough preacher, when in actuality over the last several months Shippensburg and Swatara Churches of God have contacted me about interviewing as possible pastor.

God called me into the ministry, He called me here and to the Chairman of Missions and Church Development. God also called me to serve the Commission on World Missions, and it is His work I must rejoice in, for being part of. I rejoice that God saw fit to use me.

It is a joy to lead the Manheim Bible Study, and I am thankful that He used me to begin High View Church. It is a given that He has said that I am acceptable to Him. I must believe Him; He has promised to empower us and lead us to do His work—and He has.

***

As an interesting recap of a week in the life of a pastor—my life—during this time, I share the following "events" as a reality check for those who may have an idealized view of being a church leader.

Monday I spoke at a funeral. People asked me, "Was this person saved?"

Tuesday I visited with a lady who found out her son never recovered from his accident of last year. I also visited a lady who had just returned from the doctor, and probably has cancer.

Wednesday I visited a man who wants to bring a woman of immoral reputation with him to church. He stays with her, or she comes and stays with him. He is still married, and doesn't seem interested in making restitution with his wife.

Thursday there was a council meeting and we discussed a problem a person has working with people, yet she was nominated to the Nominating Committee. Who do we select to be the sixth member of Commission on Missions and Church Development?

On Friday, the moving of the missionary trailer was cancelled again. I am responsible. How much of the load can I carry?

I checked on the price of plane tickets for missionaries. I visited with a man on prednisone; he is not well.

Friday, I sat down for a leisure evening and received a call from a lady telling me that a man of the church had been telling people that I said she was "psychopathic." She questioned me as to why I was against her.

I received a letter that day from a lady asking me to help a man, however this man and his family doesn't want any help.

On Saturday, I visited a man who accepted Christ; his family doesn't attend church.

The easiest thing I did this week was get a haircut.

After visiting others, we went out to celebrate an anniversary dinner with some friends.

Dad's health has been failing; had a blood transfusion this week, and he seems very tired.

I preached twice on Sunday (1 Thessalonians 4:1-12) on sexual immorality; then on Sunday evening had communion service and preached about feet washing.

On Monday, the trailer move was cancelled again. I then reviewed names for mission pastors. A mission pastor called about a violence problem in his church. I received several other calls concerning other members of the church.

I need to pray and spend some time in God's Word. I have been reading 1 Thessalonians for several weeks. It is a book of the Bible well worth reading and absorbing.

****

Part III
Perilous Times

But mark this: ***There will be terrible times in the last days****. People will be lovers of themselves, lovers of money, boastful, proud, abusive, disobedient to their parents, ungrateful, unholy, without love, unforgiving, slanderous, without self-control, brutal, not lovers of the good, treacherous, rash, conceited, lovers of pleasure rather than lovers of God—having a form of godliness but denying its power.* ***Have nothing to do with such people.***

(2 Timothy 3:1-5 NIV)

****

15
The Cost of Suffering

Although I didn't have much time for politics, at home or abroad, I did kept an eye and ear on news from Haiti as often as time allowed. The president for life, Baby Doc, was in it for himself. He was a playboy who squandered money that the citizens needed to survive.

By the mid-1980s, the situation in Haiti was becoming critical, and a period of unsafe travel to the island nation was just around the corner, severely limiting my ability to lend my support to the Haitian people in person, which was my passion.

I watched in horror from our home in Lancaster County, Pennsylvania, as violent rioters and looters feverishly took to the streets of Port-au-Prince. As I saw the angry retaliation against the Tonton Macoute, I wondered if my friend Felix was among those who had been tortured and killed. Felix, after all, had obvious connections to the government—to be an official of the Duvalier regime, whether currently or formerly, now meant having a target on your back.

The Duvaliers settled in Talloires, France, and for a short while continued to live in luxury. In the aftermath of Duvalier's departure, the Legislative Chamber and Duvalier's armed forces, Volontaire Sécurité Nationale, was dissolved, signaling the end of the Tonton Macoute.

However, it was soon obvious that a new militant administration would pick up where the previous regime left off. The National Council of Government (Conseil National de Gouvernement, CNG) was soon established, led by General Henri Namphy. Namphy became president of the interim governing council, made up of six civilian and military members, which promised elections and democratic reforms. However, it wasn't long before his regime was publicly labeled as "Duvalierism without Duvalier." What appeared as a hopeful new beginning, was now looking like more of the same corruption and violence.

However, a Catholic priest and an outspoken critic of Duvalierism, Jean-Bertrand Aristide, had begun making a name for himself. An exponent of Liberation Theology, Aristide had denounced Duvalier's regime in one of his first public sermons. This did not go unnoticed by the regime's top echelons, and Aristide would be forced into exile in Montreal, Canada. He was famously quoted for preaching, "The path of those Haitians who reject the regime is the path of righteousness and love." By the end of the decade, Aristide traded his priestly pulpit for a political podium.

From our home in Pennsylvania, I was helpless to do much at all, as travel to Haiti had become too dangerous. The years following Baby Doc's departure were riddled with more unrest, corrupt elections, and citizen backlash against a government fighting to remain more militant than democratic. My hope of seeing Haiti won for Christ was slipping away.

At home, my father's health declined beyond recovery, and my church body, like many churches throughout America, continued to lose its fire for the Lord.

***

> *"I know your deeds, that you are neither cold nor hot. I wish you were either one or the other! So, because you are lukewarm—neither hot nor cold—I am about to spit you out of my mouth. You say, 'I am rich; I have acquired wealth and do not need a thing.' But you do not realize that you are wretched, pitiful, poor, blind and naked. I counsel you to buy from me gold refined in the fire, so you can become rich; and white clothes to wear, so you can cover your shameful nakedness; and salve to put on your eyes, so you can see.*
>
> *"Those whom I love I rebuke and discipline. So be earnest and repent. Here I am! I stand at the door and knock. If anyone hears my voice and opens the door, I will come in and eat with that person, and they with me.*
>
> *"To the one who is victorious, I will give the right to sit with me on my throne, just as I was victorious and sat down with my Father on his throne. Whoever has ears, let them hear what the Spirit says to the churches"* (Revelation 3:15-22 NIV).

These last ten years since we returned from Haiti have deadened my spirit. I seem to be no longer burdened for the lost, no longer driven to my knees in prayer. I no longer have the great desire to study the Bible. Preparing sermons is a struggle. Is it because I don't think people will listen and be changed, or that I don't see results anymore?

Evangelism was once the goal of my life. What is wrong now? I seem to be just like those around me—concerned for myself, not concerned for the unsaved.

Missions were once my main priority, but not so anymore. Is it because of what I have seen and experienced? I don't find many of the main church people interested in bringing the lost to Jesus, concerned for church growth, or loving new and/or different people. Preaching seems like an exercise in futility.

Oh, to have the presence and power of God at work in my life and in the church. Oh, to be at peace with God, to be at rest and not be harassed by all I see happening in the church. Some mornings when I awake, it seems as if my well has gone dry.

Dad hemorrhaged for the past six days and is at Hershey Medical Center. He just wants to rest. How do I deal with these times in my life? It is hard, to say the least. How much should a man have to go through? How do we deal with modern medicine's idea that they can "fix anything"? What about the cost of human suffering, just to be "fixed up" for a few more days of suffering? It is not God who determines life and death?

It was difficult to come home from Hershey last evening and then preach the Maundy Thursday Communion Service. I realize a lifetime is a short time; Dad may be 70, but I am only 24 years off of that. It makes me think about life and what really counts. I doubt if it is expensive cars, owning property, or elaborate caskets.

Lord, help me to be Christian in all the days ahead. Don't let my mind be on the little things.

There is a question in my mind as I think of the upcoming congregational meeting. I don't know what to expect after ten years of serving God. But I do know that God is sovereign and still on His throne. I will trust in Him.

***

> *Jesus told her, "I am the resurrection and the life. Anyone who believes in me will live, even after dying"* (John 11:25 NLT).
>
> *"O death, where is your victory? O death, where is your sting?" ...But thank God! He gives us victory over sin and death through our Lord Jesus Christ* (1 Corinthians 15:55,57 NLT).

I woke that morning with the feeling Dad would not be with us much longer. He passed a few days later. Life is from crisis to crisis; Dad's death was a blow, but nothing like the blow of my sister-in-law wanting to leave my brother-in-law. I was at such a loss to know how to think or feel. I feel angry, sad, deceived or let down and disappointed. I don't know how to react to this situation. I'm frustrated that six weeks of counseling did not help her change her mind. Why do people pretend all is well rather than confess their sin?

My commitment for missions has waned. I need to get my eyes on Jesus, not people. I must allow the Holy Spirit to minister to me as the Comforter. People will always be disappointing in one way or the other—but God…

Lord, I need to keep my mind open to Your will; it is hard to know what to do, we are not making any progress here, attendance is down. I question if we should move, but I am fearful that I will not be a success if we move to another church. Will the next church be the same? I think of starting a mission church, but would that fail?

Lord, I need Your leading; I don't know what to do.

****

16
Planning and Planting

Oh what a difference a year makes in my life. I could live here in Lancaster County and be very comfortable—in that not much is expected of me. The church is well pleased with what I'm doing and not interested in doing more or starting new projects. Although I could live here comfortably till I died, I don't have the peace of God. There must be a difference between comfort and God's will.

I had the desire to plant more churches and offer more elective classes in Sunday school and Wednesday evenings. I had tried to get the church to create more spaces so we could have more options for new groups. I still believe the church should offer counseling for those who are struggling. To offer more electives on parenting, marriage, finances, how to be sure you're a Christian, how to experience God's love and forgiveness, and how to disciple people to become followers of Christ.

But the church was very happy the way it was and didn't see any reason for change or adding new programs. Although I was chomping at the bit for change, and to add to what we were presently doing, I resigned myself to the fact that the people couldn't be coerced into more than they were ready to accept.

So, I focused my efforts toward planting a church in Willow Street, Pennsylvania; an unincorporated and census-designated community in Lancaster County, Pennsylvania, with a population less than 8,000.

***

Thinking back about planning and planting I remember that back in 1961, Junior Grissinger and I rented the Downin Farm. When we divided it, Junior picked the half he wanted and I took the other half. He picked all the slate land that was the easiest to plow and plant; giving me the stony land that was hard to plow and work.

We had a drought that summer, all the slate dried out and the corn crop was very poor. However, the stony soil held the moisture much better and I had a very good crop. Lesson learned: ***plow stony ground, it grows better corn.***

There are times when loneliness and rejection are hard to bear. When I see men prosper who never took a stand for right, who only sought popularity and fame, who did the safe thing, not the right thing, I ask God to show me His will and destiny for my life. The issue of abortion and church views especially stir my emotions. Some churches and preachers do not speak out about death and evil because they could lose their tax-exempt status. Jesus preached and taught the truth, the heck with tax and money concerns. Does preaching the truth that Jesus taught (Sermon on the Mount) make us unacceptable to the church as a pastor?

When we do well, when we are righteous and honest, God may be the only one who sees. And that is enough. Doing well is sometimes the only reward we receive. Perhaps we should not expect any reward in this life. Doing well is its own reward.

***

Yet, again I am haunted by my wonderings: *What if I would have tried harder. What if I would have pushed more? Oh God, what if I would've split the church? If Your Holy Spirit doesn't move people, should I try to do it in the energy of the flesh? Lord, I have tried to do everything the Spirit led me to do, everything I knew to do. Is this the truth or is it a cop out? Lord, how do I close this chapter and commit it to Your grace?*

For the last year, every day I have felt burdened that we must work toward goals. Am I misled to believe these goals are important? Who is right about the goals, the church leaders or me? What is God's goal?

We have been here for a quarter of my life and all of our youngest son Jamie's life. It is not easy to leave, but it doesn't seem good for the church or me to stay. I need to see progress—the church is happy as is.

Lord, I thank and praise You for what You have done at High View through those who were called and made the commitment by faith, long before it was popular to do so. Lord, I rejoice when I think of Manheim, and that handful of people who stepped out in faith, believing You would raise up a church there.

Lord, these last months would have been very frustrating and seemed like a waste if it was not for the fellowship of those You have called to pay any required price to see a church planted in Willow Street, Pennsylvania.

Oh God, it is a humbling experience to see a few people, who have such faith that they know that someday they will be Your church in Willow Street. Lord, it is exciting to see people respond to Your call, when it can be hard to do so—when there is opposition and lack of support. Oh God, give them faith equal to the task. May no tears be too bitter or no cost too great to see lost people in Heaven. May we share not only the Gospel of God, but our lives as well! (See 1 Thessalonians 2:6.)

It is hard for me to understand how a few people have the commitment to plant, and I know they do, when so many in the existing church don't have the faith, commitment, or willingness to do any of the things that would help the church grow and for people to be saved.

***

I've learned over the years that I can't do or accomplish what God or the Holy Spirit can't do with people. An example: it's one thing to counsel and encourage people who have an addiction. But if they will not listen to Jesus and obey Him, I have no ability to force them to change and be delivered.

With God's help, I can set goals, preach, and teach. I can do my best to lead the congregation. But if they don't have a mind to listen to the leading of the Holy Spirit, a pastor can't force them to do anything they don't want to do. We are blessed with a "free will" to make decisions—right or wrong. So, if Jesus can't convince people, no one else can.

Ultimately, there was lack of support, so the Willow Street church plant never took root. We tried and failed—but at least we tried. To me it was well worth the effort; no matter the cost to plant churches or to open a mission field or start a new elective class or small group. It's worth the cost to try to reach people for Jesus Christ, even if some reject the Gospel.

Jesus' disciples constantly faced opposition and persecution but they continued to be faithful to the call of God.

> *When I am with those who are weak, I share their weakness, for I want to bring the weak to Christ. Yes, I try to find common ground with everyone, doing everything I can to save some. I do everything to spread the Good News and share in its blessings* (1 Corinthians 9:22-23 NLT).

***

I was called to lead in my home church. I was called to be a missionary to Haiti and to help open the work there. I was called to be a pastor. I was called to be a church planter, to go and make disciples. None of these things were ever easy. But I still believe with all my heart that they are what God called me to do. Now I believe in my old age that God has called me to share in the celebrate recovery program at New Providence Church of God. What a blessing!

***

> *I lift up my eyes to the mountains—where does my help come from? My help comes from the Lord, the Maker of heaven and earth* (Psalm 121:1-2 NIV).

In 1988 I accepted a pastor position in Newburg, Pennsylvania, a small community near Shippensburg in Cumberland County. The views of the Blue and North mountains is inspiring here and the lush rolling fields full of corn and dairy cows always makes me smile.

It has been easy to preach here; Dolores started a Ladies Bible Study. I needed to learn how the system works, which was different from other churches. The pastor picks the nominating committee; the pastor makes the decisions for the Missionary Board, the Sunday school classes, Rally Day, Living Christmas Tree, and even the council. When I suggested that the group make decisions, they continued to wait on my input or instructions. Thankfully, I made some headway by establishing a Mission Conference and choosing a new Living Christmas tree director and new choir director.

The people are helpful and faithful—they appreciate sharing ideas and are given the opportunity to speak out, but some are either reluctant to take charge or they take charge and don't regard any other authority. Everything is done or managed by one person, not a board or committee. That person does his own thing without telling anyone else what he is doing. I need to get used to this system. It is like a conference with many separate churches, each one doing their own thing. The youth, junior and primary churches, bus ministry, bus captains, youth director, sport teams and yes, I suppose the pastor also. Pastoral leadership is crucial here to work with all the groups.

***

In 1990, the Sunday school attendance was down 65 compared to a year ago on the same day. It is hard for me to be positive. As is my habit, I started questioning myself: Is it my fault the attendance was dropping? How much more will it drop? It's those who were manipulated and persuaded to attend in the past are no longer attending, right? Whose image am I fighting to protect? If the people had been saved and were discipled, would they have quit?

Lord, help me to forget the past and to start over with new people, new prospects, new ideas and new programs. Lord, what do You want me to do here at Newburg? I feel like a little child and I don't know what to do; unless You tell me or give me wisdom. I have no answer or vision. And unless I have a vision, I can't lead. Lord, this is Your church, so please tell me what to do because I don't know.

The Lord told me to call one elder, one deacon, and one deaconess and ask each one to call the others and prayerfully consider how to be more effective in prayer for revival and promotion of the revival. It's great how people can think when they are led to think. Thank You, Lord!

Yesterday at a ministerial meeting, a man spoke on leadership and management. Pastors are to lead not manage; leaders present vision, managers take care of operations. Have I been too busy managing that I have no time to pray, study, and hear from God?

What does God want us to do here at Newburg? Is it more important to do the ministry or to equip the church for the work of ministry? Am I a leader? Do I need training? Do I just need the courage to lead? Am I afraid of the outcome of being responsible?

I seem to always have more questions than answers.

Thankfully God has every answer to every question. On that I can always and forever depend!

****

17
Facing Reality

In the 1990s, I took students from Winebrenner Seminary to Haiti for a week and showed them how the country really was geographically, politically, economically, and spiritually. I also took the commission members one year so they could see firsthand how the missionaries worked and lived. I also conducted a week-long conference on evangelism, where we actually went out and put the techniques into practice. A youth retreat on the beach one year was also a success. We visited a Haitian village way up in the mountains where there was a Church of God. It was the scene of some kind of land, taxation, or water rights issue and many houses in the village had been burned and people killed.

Politically:

> On September 30, 1991, a military coup under the leadership of Lieutenant General Raoul Cedras overthrew the government of Jean-Bertrand Aristide, the first popularly elected president in Haitian history. President George H.W. Bush called for the restoration of democracy, and worked with the Organization of American States (OAS) to impose a trade embargo on all goods except medicine and food. During his 1992 presidential candidacy, Bill Clinton criticized the Bush administration for its policy on refugee return and promised to increase pressure on the military junta by tightening economic sanctions.
>
> ...With military action clearly imminent, former President Jimmy Carter led a delegation to Haiti in search of a negotiated settlement. Carter, Senator Sam Nunn, and General Colin Powell flew to Haiti on September 17, well aware that they had little time to reach agreement. President Clinton approved Carter's mission, but insisted that the military operation would proceed as scheduled. The invasion forces launched with the negotiations in progress, without any certainty whether they would make an opposed or a peaceful entry on to Haitian soil.
>
> The Haitian leadership capitulated in time to avoid bloodshed. Having launched the operation with the expectation of a forced-

entry assault, the forces conducting the operation displayed remarkable discipline and flexibility in adjusting to this new and uncertain environment. General Hugh Shelton, commander of the invasion force, was transformed enroute to Haiti from commander to diplomat, charged with working out a peaceful transition of power. Shelton and Cedras met on September 20, 1994, to begin the process, and Aristide returned to Haiti on October 15.[1]

***

I believe there are often two spirits at work in us. One is the Spirit of almighty God. The other is the spirit selfishness and arrogance; of wanting what we want rather than wanting what God wants.

With that said, what is there left to say? Didn't Job say it all? (See especially Job 1:20-22.) I have gone through experiences that I have wondered if anybody understood or cared. I have been to the depth of despair; I have even despaired of life itself. It has seemed that I am despised, rejected, and worthless. I have been totally out of touch with reality.

Thank God someone came along side me to tell me that I am a man of God, doing God's will. It saved me when I could see that my value and worth is measured by God and not human standards, achievements, and the world's acceptance. I am accepted by HIM (God) even if everybody else rejects me and if by the world's standards I'm a failure.

The days go so fast and I seem to be too busy to write, think, or pray. I get caught up in the success syndrome and measuring myself with others. I wish I could face the reality of knowing that God's evaluation of me is all that matters; even my own evaluation of me doesn't matter—especially so!

***

All the boys and I laid up the blocks for the corner of the barn. They were so cooperative and worked together to get it completed that night even though I had to leave. They did a great job. It looks real nice; they do nice work, even if I am their father. We had a wonderful meal with friends.

God has blessed our family with His love and grace throughout the years. We have also been blessed with friends from around the world. How can I ever doubt His goodness and His faithfulness? I don't doubt it. I love it!

***

The Newburg church started having two services on Sunday mornings; after a while there was opposition that caused the future of the second service to be in doubt. I believed that multiple services were a good thing as we reached more people and people had a second time option.

The Lord is the head of the church and if He can't lead it to be more fruitful, there is no chance that I can. I could see the opposition building, and it was obvious I needed to depend on the clear leading of God and not lean on my own understanding regarding the simmering conflict.

I prayed a lot during that time: Lord, You are the Head of the church. Help me not to usurp Your position. You will build Your church and the gates of hell will not overcome it (Matthew 16:18). Lord, help me to depend on You, not people. I ask You, Lord, for a spirit of discernment. Help me to know when to keep my mouth shut, and when to let You fight the battles.

I believe firmly that God will vindicate the righteous (Psalm 35:24). The only thing that counts when we are planted is if we were good "seed." If we were, there will be a great harvest from our life (see James 3:18).

***

Our son Kevin turned 22 on July 24, 1992. Those years passed so quickly—unlike the previous six months of continual stress. I'm so tired. Nevertheless, God has been so good. His people have been so faithful. In my worst times, I have been supported, encouraged and loved. At times, it seemed it would be my last day. Every day seems to bring more persecution. I am haunted again, day and night, that I might fail. Today, I don't have much hope. But…the Lord has been faithful and I believe He will be faithful in the future. I pray Thy will be done. Amen!

***

In September 1992, I met with all of the elders on a Sunday night and we discussed making progress regarding the conflict. One of the elders wanted to meet me the next morning. I agreed. When we met, he said he came to tell me I was fired. The church board gave me a two month sabbatical and brought an interim that was supposed to work on resolving the issues. His recommendation to them was to fire me rather than work together.

My family was very supportive they knew how hard I had worked and they knew how wrong many of the accusations were. My friends and many from the congregation, rallied around to pray for me and to support us.

One man who had a great impact on me was a judge. He publicly told the denomination and the congregation that no one in his courtroom was ever accused without having the opportunity to present the evidence. He ask them to please present any evidence they had of wrongdoing on my part. He asked them to do so in a congregational meeting, where I was supposed to stand up front and hear their accusations.

All the leaders stated they were not at liberty to disclose any details, or who told them they had promised to keep all of the accusations secret, and not tell anyone where the accusations came from or who made the accusations.

***

The Lord gave me as a sermon topic Matthew 5:44, where Jesus said:

Love your enemies.
Do good to those who hate you.
Bless those who curse you.
Pray for those who persecute you or mistreat you.

The burden was no longer on my shoulders.

***

This was a first for me; being fired.

Shortly afterward, Dolores and I attended a service at Harvey Cedars and heard a sermon preached on Elijah giving up. Those gathered were asked how many felt like giving up, but wanted to rededicate their lives to serve the Lord. Dolores and I responded.

That same week, I wrote each of our four boys a letter, sharing what the Lord had done in my life and encouraged them to serve the Lord through it all. As apostle Paul wrote, *"For I am already being poured out like a drink offering, and the time for my departure is near. I have fought the good fight, I have finished the race, I have kept the faith"* (2 Timothy 4:6-7 NIV).

My last Sunday to preach the hurt was so bad I could hardly stand up. I preached "Religious but Lost"; three roads people take:

- Popular Road (Matthew 7:13-14)
- Religious Road (Matthew 7:21-23)
- Easy Road (Matthew 7:24-27)

My last sermon was the greatest sermon ever preached—because it was preached by the greatest Preacher who ever preached, the carpenter from Nazareth, Jesus was His name. It is recorded in Matthew chapters 5, 6, and 7; I read it word for word. You could have heard a pin drop; people were glued to their Bibles, listening to every word. God is good. What a blessing this was to us; praise the Lord! Jesus said, *"I send you out as sheep in the midst of wolves"* (Matthew 10:16 NKJV), and do not be afraid of people (Matthew 10:26).

The other day I read Acts 7:60 (NIV), the dying words of Stephen, *"Lord, do not hold this sin against them."* And he died. That is being Christlike.

***

In the first 24 hours, I realized that the church could go on without me and that I could go on without being responsible for the church. Jesus is responsible for the church. I can sleep, go away all day or take a two-week vacation, and the church will survive. My promise is to never again take on the responsibilities for a church, the people, or elected officials. That is a sin against Jesus to feel His church can't make it without my input.

Lord, I want to be holy, not successful, to be godly not religious. I want to do Your will, not mine or other people's wills. I want to serve You, not You serve me. I want to worship Your majesty, not my own might. Know You and the power of Your resurrection, not my own strength. I want You to live through me, not me living through my own power. Glorify You, not make my own name important.

> *We give thanks to You, O God, we give thanks! For Your wondrous works declare that Your name is near. ...But God is the Judge: He puts down one, and exalts another* (Psalm 75:1,7 NKJV).

Note
1. "Intervention in Haiti, 1994-1995," Office of the Historian, Department of State, USA; https://history.state.gov/milestones/1993-2000/haiti; accessed September 2, 2021.

****

18
Looking Back

The following is the letter written to each of my sons that I mentioned in the previous chapter:

September 4, 1992

Dear Son:

As I look back over my life, the thing that makes me happiest is to see what you, my son, have become. I am indeed grateful for what you are and what you will be by the grace of your God and mine. I praise the Lord for you.

As your mother and I wait on God for what we shall do next, I have had an opportunity to think back over my life and see what God has done. It is hard for me to imagine that God would speak to me, a timid 15-year-old farm boy, and call me to commit my life to follow Jesus wherever it would lead and whatever it cost. Truly I never had any idea where all God would call and lead me.

All my life I had a passion to farm and loved cows. I lived to farm. If the farm and cows were ever to be sold, I thought that it would be over my dead body. But when God called me to Haiti, one of the most natural things on earth was to sell the cows and farm. It just seemed as natural as it is for a mother who has carried a baby for nine months to give birth.

It overwhelms me to think of how the Lord has called and led me through life.

It was God who led me into the hell called Haiti. And it was God who led me all the way. I thank Him for the churches that were planted and the lives that were changed and people who were encouraged.

It was not my idea to go where tens of thousands were cruelly persecuted and executed for political purpose and power, where voodoo drums beat all night long; where there was darkness and terror; where I couldn't speak a word of Creole, where I was often alone and at their mercy. God did it. He led me all the way.

I was always shy, afraid of the dark, fearful of people, especially people who were not like me, afraid to fly, and of cities. Can you imagine me alone in an alien country looking down the wrong end of a gun barrels held by black men? That was not much worse for me than being the pastor of five churches on the Walnut Grove Charge. I was assigned to preach there before I had taken even one of the 63 courses in the ministerial study course.

I—who was afraid to say "hi" to someone I met on the road to Maddensville or take an "F" before I would stand in front of the class and speak—was now preaching in five churches. It was not by my desire or strength, but by the grace of God. Neither was it my desire to go to New Providence. Nor was it by my ability that I was able to stay there for twelve years.

Everything that God has called me to do, I was afraid to do. I was not prepared to do; never felt adequately trained and never felt capable, every job always seemed more than I thought I could handle. As I look back at everything in my life, it is because of God.

When I think about it, it's a miracle to survive over four years and preach over 500 sermons to people; some of them were hit right between the eyes with many of the sermons God gave me to share. How long will people put up with preaching that they don't want to hear and obey? I don't know what the future holds for us; but I sure do know that the One who holds the future is the same One who had led us all the way.

As I think back, many things come to my mind as to how I hurt your feelings and wounded your spirit, offended or disappointed you. Please forgive me.

When I look back, I can see many things that I should have done differently. I am ashamed that I did not have the needed insight or patience to listen more.

I hope that my testimony encourages you to trust God always. For He has never let me down and He will never let you down. He can do immeasurably more than you can ever ask, think, or imagine. I am proud of you and your family, in the way you live your life.

I love you,
Dad

***

I sent this letter to each of our four sons. They were very supportive of us when we had to leave the Newburg Church of God. All of them are faithful to Jesus Christ today and are raising godly children. Praise God!

***

October 1992 brought with it warm, fall-like sunshine and the wonderful task of picking corn—there were 14 acres to pick! *What a day,* I thought, *it will be when my Jesus I shall see and He asks me what I've done.*

I saw a man who encouraged me not to give up, not to quit preaching. "Sinful men need the Gospel," he said. He gave me the New Testament to read that I gave him when he was saved. He had written some important truths in the margins:

- *Fear is the opposite of faith.*
- *Everyone who hears you; may be hearing you for the last time.*
- *Pardon for the past, power for the present, prospect for the future.*
- *The heavenly Father chose me for the same reason He chose Abraham; to live His truth, to enjoy His world, and to pass His plan for our lives on to others.*
- *Everyone is standing between someone and hell.*
- *You may be the only one standing between another person and hell.*

Other lessons learned:

Twenty years from now, I want to leave behind a multitude of trained disciples involved in ministry; everyone using their spiritual gifts. Not a huge building that uses up the Lord's money for heat, lights, and upkeep.

I'd rather have Jesus than anything; I want Jesus more than anything. Jesus calls us to go and make disciples. He sent out the disciples and the 70 to do ministry.

Be Christlike, before attempting to do the work of Christ.

Christ must live in me, before I witness to anyone about Christ. Stand up for Jesus before you speak; there is already too many people speaking for Jesus, who neither live for nor stand up for Jesus when it is dangerous or costly.

Jesus died for us that we may by faith believe on Him, obey Him, follow Him, no matter what the cost, no matter where it takes us, or when He calls. Jesus didn't call us to build temples or make church members; but to make disciples.

When I die, what a day that will be, when my Jesus I shall see and I look up on His face and He asks me, how many disciples did you make who are serving Me?

***

I seemed happy and content for times throughout my life. Was I? Yes, I was humbly proud of myself because I realized I had done the right thing. I was not always depressed or angry. I had done the right thing and I was proud of the stands I took over the years for my Savior. God has blessed and provided for my family and me. I am taken care of wonderfully in my old age. Jesus kept the promise He made when He said whoever gives up houses and lands…He will bless.

We will never regret anything we give up for the cause of Christ. I sold my dream farm, the herd of cattle I started raising when I was a young boy, to go to Haiti on a mission there. It is still in operation to this day. In 2008 I helped start another mission work in Haiti.

And how does one make disciples? Jesus said go and make disciples by teaching them to obey all that I have commanded.

***

January 28, 1993

Looking back, it was painful for me to take my ordination certificate down off the wall and file it away. Too much of my worth was based on work and accomplishments. I needed to focus on the grace of God that is more than adequate. Considering all that God did for me and my family over the years, I still find it so horrific what people can do to each other. When reading biographies of Christians, it is fascinating what some have overcome and how tenacious they were to stand strong for their faith.

Some people can be jealous, envious, greedy, selfish, and lust for more and more. Why do they take advantage and deceive people? Why do people want to take from others? Why do people want to take someone's earned pay, possessions or property, even food and clothing? Why don't people help rather than take?

Oh, God! Some days I long for Your day of reckoning to hasten. Please God help me to understand. God, help me to recognize evil, not be blinded or surprised by it, or become overly despondent because of evil. Lord, I don't know how to deal with this corrupt and dishonest world filled with crooks and liars.

I turned briefly to selling real estate. Yet again I allowed people to deceive me into thinking they were good, honest, and moral people. Why do I give people the benefit of the doubt? Why do I accept people at face value and never doubt or question them? I'd like to think it's because I'm trying to reflect the compassion of Jesus. But even He said to be, *"wise as serpents and harmless as doves"* (Matthew 10:16 NKJV).

Never discount the obvious.

***

There were certainly evildoers in Haiti—in the highest government offices to the looters on the roadways. But I have the most difficult time understanding the evil done in the name of religion.

I have read about the German holocaust and was astonished how such a tragedy could ever happen. Some people can feign goodness and religion and justify any evil when they believe there is some benefit in it for them.

Many of the German people were religious and educated; multitudes could have resisted, rebelled, spoke up, but instead valued their own lives more than righteousness and the common good. Fear and selfishness are powerful motivators. Would I have had the courage to stand up and speak out when it meant death? The answer is to the question, "How do I stand up now to evil in everyday events?" Either God controls your life or self does; many are the religious whose lives are controlled by selfishness.

Dietrich Bonhoeffer, a German pastor and anti-Nazi dissident said, "Faith is only real when there is obedience, never without it, and faith only becomes faith in the act of obedience."[1] He was one of the few who stood up when it counted. How many people do you know stand up when it really counts?

***

What I have left is family, friends and what is eternal. My bank account may be down to zero and I may be in debt, but I know in my heart I have tried to treat people fairly and honestly. There are some things that people can't take from us—changed lives are eternal, God is keeping score. Thank You, God.

There go I but for the grace of God (see 1 Corinthians 15:10).

***

When I was 53 years old in 1993, I was a real estate agent to support Dolores and I and also still be involved in missions and church planting. While I was in the Chambersburg area working, three different groups of immigrants came to me and said they needed a church building. I helped. Immigrants don't usually have resources or money for a new church, so I set them up with an installment sales contract, so they could buy a building without having to go through the commercial lending process.

Haitians and Hispanics were very interested in planting churches and I was very interested in planting churches as well, so my job and my calling worked together. God is so good! I soon was connected with more and more immigrants interested in starting a church. A lot were Hispanic or Latino, and many from Guatemala.

Note
1. Deitrich Bonhoeffer, *The Cost of Discipleship* (New York: SCM press Ltd., 1959, Touchstone, 2018).

****

19
Pleasing God or Pleasing People

One January morning in 1994, the sun wasn't up yet, but my mind was awake and thinking how our nation of the United States could fall into such sinful depravity by covering up sin and refusing to stand up for what is right. As I looked back at the events between the U.S. and Haiti, I still can't understand how most people can go along with evil—as long as they personally are not affected. Is there no sense of right and wrong that is stronger than self-preservation? The worst dysfunction is to cover sin and call evil right.

Oh Lord, I don't know what to do, or where to find work. I know that where I am now is not the right place. I will wait patiently on You, Lord, for where You want to lead me. Lord, I need a job and to sell my lots, and there is not one thing I can do to hasten either.

Lord, I commit this day and my needs to You. Help me to forget and forgive, to leave the past, and stop fighting the battle. Lord, help me to start living in today and anticipating the future. I need to stop thinking that the future will be like the past; that is not FAITH!

Faith is keeping on when all goes wrong. Faith is keeping your chin up when there is nothing to be happy about. I search to know the way to go; I am called to preach, but sick of the Pharisees in the church. I love to farm; but I don't know how to start over again. The real estate business is so uncertain, there are months with no pay.

I am taking my transcripts to the United Brethren in Christ Church in hopes of finding a pastoring position. I have a problem trusting people; I am growing weary in the struggle. There is politics in everything—even in the churches—but politics is not everything.

Who do I trust? Not everyone is trustworthy. When I see signs of dishonesty, I take them to heart. If things don't add up, I face reality. If I have a doubt about someone, I don't trust the person. Don't ever discount the obvious is a good tip I've learned from the Lord.

People are what they are—and when the pressure is on, that's when real character is revealed. Even Christians have been a disappointment to me—but God never lets me down.

In some circles, Christianity has become more of a symbol than a reality; church more of a club than a House of God. It is sad when the world can't tell who is a Christian and who isn't. Many people are saved, but not converted to God's way of thinking and living. Many have no clear set of convictions, morals, or standards. Righteousness or holiness is not a concept they understand. Is it any wonder the next generation is not interested in their brand of Christianity?

What we truly believe is what we are willing to stand up for when it is costly or dangerous to do so; when it costs friendship, security, position, prominence, reputation, job, money. When left alone, destitute, stripped of your future and few seem to care, that is when our true selves either stand or stumble. God is with us either way—our trust must always and only be in Him.

One evening in September 1994, we heard a presentation by Max McLean[1] who recited the book of Acts. Nothing has touched my heart in a long time like this reading. Peter, James, and Paul spoke as the Holy Spirit gave them the message. They were threatened, beaten, put in jail, driven out of town, chased from city to city. They obeyed God rather than man. They spoke on behalf of the Holy Spirit; they defied the church leaders and the government. They were unlearned men, but they knew the Sovereign God and the resurrected Christ. They preached and testified with tremendous power. These men confronted the (religious) church; they were God-called men, and they knew the God who called them.

It was not ordination and degrees that drove the apostles to suffer persecution. It was not the religious who encouraged them to press on and to speak out, never to be silenced, never to give up or quit. They confronted religion, they questioned, they disagreed, they preached, they divided and disrupted the pious and religious hierarchy.

Why don't seminaries teach this stance of standing strong for their faith? Why?

Why don't churches teach people more about Peter, James, Paul, Deitrich Bonhoeffer, Amy Carmichael, David Livingstone, Hudson Taylor, Francis Schaeffer, William Tyndale, James Dobson, Jim Elliott, Nate Saint, and Billy Graham? And organizations like Wycliffe that has translated the Bible into more than 3,000 languages worldwide.

Have we forgotten, or did we ever really know or study, great men of faith such as John Huss (Jan Hus), John Winebrenner, Martin Luther, and Pastor Richard Wurmbrand from Romania who defied the Soviet Union and helped cause Communism to fall in his country?

Who am I following? Am I truly and solely following my Sovereign God, Creator of Heaven and earth—or selfish men and women, biased church hierarchy, and corrupt government officials?

Am I a follower of the resurrected Christ, the persecuted One, the Crucified, the One who never flinched, and the One who faced Calvary defiantly worshipping His Father rather than human rulers? Am I worthy to suffer persecution as the disciple of the Crucified One?

Should I have obeyed men rather than God? Did I do the right thing? If I did right, then I am right. But in this world's eyes it doesn't seem right. This world's system says a man is spiritual if his church grows, builds, and has a large budget, if he is respected no matter the issues that affect the honor of God, no matter if he doesn't take a stand on God's behalf.

According to today's church, Paul, James, Peter, John, and hundreds more down to Bonhoeffer and others are and were not successful. Am I concerned by the success measured by men and religion, or God? Is it better to be judged successful by men or God? I know the answer—you do too.

Have we—you, me, the church—forgotten that God would rather have righteousness than religious ritual, burnt sacrifices? (See Hosea 6:6; Matthew 9:13; Mark 12:33 NKJV.) Am I a disciple of Christ according to the book of Acts?

Are we taught to uphold and promote a religion or denomination rather than the Sovereign God, the crucified and resurrected Lord? What do churches and seminaries teach? What do we practice? What does the world see? What does the world see in me? What does God see?

***

If Noah was a righteous man, why wasn't there hundreds or thousands of people following him into the ark?

In Acts 2, Peter had 3,000 followers. In Acts 4, Peter and John are before the council; and in Acts 4:18, they were told not to speak, to stop speaking about Jesus. They had to decide which was right; obey man or obey God. They could not stop speaking about what they had seen and heard about the Son of God. In Acts 4:21, they were warned strongly to stop—immediately, though, they gathered together to pray for boldness to preach.

Have I been bold enough? Have I done enough? Have I spoken up for God? Have I pleased God or man? Have I stood up for righteousness; have I been depressed because I am dependent on the approval of man, rather than God? Or even more dependent upon ordination than the Holy Spirit, more dependent on success than righteousness?

***

I have tried to obey God; going to Haiti was an act of obedience to God. I didn't want to sell the cows and farm and go into the scary unknown with our young sons, Jeff and Kirby. Then when I was there, I didn't want to leave, but was led by the Holy Spirit to do the right thing, even if we never went back to Haiti.

I was threatened many times and the Commission threatened me also. We came home to face the shame of people questioning, "Why are you back home?" "Didn't you go for a lifetime?" We felt it better to obey God and to speak, even if it brought us threats and shame and disgrace.

It was fearful to come home from Haiti and begin to pastor the Walnut Grove charge of five churches. It was hard to speak up and to be opposed on so many things, sometimes it was friends and relatives who opposed me. I guess ministry is supposed to be hard. The devil can always find someone to come against and oppose the Gospel.

It would have been easier to cave in or give in than to stand up at Cherry Grove and to be opposed by even our friends.

It was painful to leave Haiti because of opposition; it was painful to leave New Providence Church of God because of their love.

***

My first priority is to live so that at least a few will thank God that I lived when my day is done. When people die, some will say, "It's good he's dead," others, more hopefully, will say, "It's good he lived among us."

Each day God provides for the next, I have only God to count on. I have nothing but my family to be "proud" of, and nothing but changed lives to show for my life's work. Only God's strength has enabled me to go on each time I was knocked down. I have discovered that I don't have to have a job; I don't have to be healthy; and I don't have to be a pastor or be ordained. All God requires of me is to be righteous.

Lord, I don't know what the future holds; all I know is that I am available to serve You. You are the God who sent Abraham across the desert, Joseph to Egypt, and David into the wilderness cave. The psalmist wrote, *"Teach us to number our days, that we may gain a heart of wisdom"* (Psalm 90:12 NKJV). Also, Psalm 39:4 (NLT) says, *"Lord, remind me how brief my time on earth will be. Remind me that my days are numbered—how fleeting my life is."* Help me to spend each day as I should. I have used up most of my days; I pray that I have used them well. I can't live them over again.

Danish writer and philosopher Soren Kierkegaard said, "Life can only be understood backwards, but it must be lived forwards." I agree.

***

Pleasing God or pleasing people is not a recent phenomenon. Even before Jesus was sent to earth the Old Testament is full of people-pleasers—as well as God-pleasers including Noah, David, Joseph, Abraham, Mary, and Esther. And in the New Testament, the same—people-pleasers and God-pleasers. None of the God-pleasers were perfect. But each were in tune with their Lord and did His bidding, obedient children of a loving Father.

Note

1. Max McLean is an award-winning actor and founder and artistic director of New York City-based Fellowship for Performing Arts. Max adapted for the stage *The Screwtape Letters, C.S. Lewis Onstage: The Most Reluctant Convert, The Great Divorce, Genesis* and *Mark's Gospel.* His recent writing and producing credits include *Martin Luther on Trial.* https://listenersbible.com/about-max-mclean/; accessed September 9, 2021.

****

20
Fighting Fear with Faith

In 1995 our financial situation was unstable but God always provided—sometimes right in the nick of time. My family was helpful and supportive. Mother loaned me money to cover part of the lots I bought in Clear Ridge and some other needs.

I thank God for the real estate job I had, knowing firsthand what it is like to be fired, black balled, and not having a job. I thank God for the many unusual ways He has provided. I settled on two pieces of mountain land that other agents said could never be sold. Because no one knew where exactly the boundary lines were, a disgruntled landowner nearby posted degrading signs about me. And the owner of the neighboring property would wave a shotgun to scare away potential buyers.

The mortgage on the land was recalled and I was given a five-day extension to produce a signed contract. There were a multitude of conditions to be satisfied. The transaction was finally settled; my commission was $4,240. I had two other settlements of $2,076—the total for two month's work. God is good. I pray He will provide listings and buyers when I need them. Selling real estate is a very insecure business, it takes faith. God give us this day our daily bread, is my prayer these days.

An old missionary spoke at our high school assembly and encouraged us to memorize:
"Seek the Kingdom of God above all else, and live righteously, and he will give you everything you need" (Matthew 6:33 NLT).

***

It seems that one way or another, I have been fighting fear with faith all my life. I chose to write this book to share what I've learned along the way. Some things I learned were free, some were costly, and others were painful. I especially want my grandchildren to know what their grandfather experienced while God gave him breath here on earth.

Also, I have learned much from other peoples' experiences. I share them so that the next generation can learn from my and other peoples' mistakes. It is also true, though, that we remember best from our own painful experiences.

Every decision in life should first of all be based on seeking the Kingdom of God above all else (see Matthew 6:33); doing so, you will avoid many heartaches and failures others experience. I have found this to be very true.

You can live a righteous life, you can obey the Lord, and you can overcome fear and temptation. You can overcome the world; you don't have to go along with the crowd when you know they are wrong. You can stand alone when you are right. You can repent, confess your sin, believe in Jesus, and go to Heaven. There is one true answer to every question, the answer is Christ.

***

What do you think? Remember, what you think controls and affects every decision of your entire life; your thoughts can predetermine your eternal destiny.

Fear keeps us from accomplishing many important things in life. Only faith can deliver us from fear. Fight fear with all the strength you have. I am a fearful person by nature. I was fearful to go to Haiti, buy a farm, buy property, land. I was very fearful to be a pastor or preach: I was fearful to pastor the Walnut Grove charge of five churches. It was fearful to move to New Providence Church of God, to leave home and the hills. I was fearful to plant the High View Church of God. The same was somewhat true with starting the Manheim Church. The fear of failure is always present for me—and most people.

I was fearful to move to Newburg Church of God, but I went with a sense of confidence from experience and having studied church growth methods. I was actually optimistic and full of faith that we could start a church in Orrstown. But after two years, if God couldn't make a church out of the congregation, I surely couldn't. It was a fearful thing to resign from Orrstown; it was the first time in 25 years I was not a pastor. At first it was a relief, and it was nice to visit our sons and other churches. But soon it felt like I was no longer needed or worthwhile.

Fear either overcomes us, or we overcome fear. Faith, the call of God, a vision from God, a personal goal, all help to overcome fear.

Fear comes in many forms, such as the fear of people, rejection, and failure. I still fear standing before a church to preach. Because of fear, many investments will never be made, many inventions never completed, many companies never started, and many books never written.

The fear of death stops many people from what they could accomplish. Astronauts have ample reasons to fear, yet they continue to blast off. The early pioneers had much to fear. I visited some old homesteads in Montana's Powder River area, the houses were very small (two rooms), water and trees almost nonexistent, rainfall 11 inches per year. How in the world did they raise enough to feed a family and protect themselves? Yet they established a homestead and survived. Some of their descendants are the hardy, self-reliant people who live and work the land in that area as of today.

Jim Elliot said, "He is no fool who gives up that which he cannot keep, to gain that which he cannot lose." On January 8, 1956, Jim and four other missionaries were killed by the Auca Indians in Ecuador—the people they had committed their lives to reaching with the good news of Jesus. A few years after the killings, though, his wife, Elisabeth, and Rachel Saint (missionary Nate Saint's sister) went to Ecuador and won to Christ the Auca tribe who had killed the men.

Nate Saint wrote the following about a month before he was killed:

> As we have a high old time this Christmas, may we who know Christ hear the cry of the damned as they hurtle headlong into Christless night without ever a chance. May we be moved with compassion as our Lord was. May we shed tears of repentance for these we have failed to bring out of darkness. Beyond the smiling scenes of Bethlehem may we see the crushing agony of Golgotha.

I have always believed that fear will keep you from the best God has to give you. If you want all God has to give—give Him all you got.

I admire the missionaries who gave their lives to spread the good news. A young man from Lancaster County, Pennsylvania, was one such man. On September 13, 1978, Chet Bitterman wrote in his diary: "…I find this recurring thought that perhaps God will call me to be martyred for him in his service in Colombia. I am willing."

On January 17, 1981, Chet told his wife, Brenda, "It's okay for someone to die for the sake of getting the word of God to the minority people of Colombia." Two days later he was taken captive and executed in Colombia.[1]

The fear of death didn't stop Chet from obeying the call of God in his life. I must truthfully admit that the fear of death and the safety of my family had a bearing on my leaving Haiti.

Is it stopping or hindering you from obeying the Lord's call to service? What is fear keeping you from doing? Being a missionary, a pastor, witnessing, ministering to those in prison, taking a new job, starting a business, investing, giving to the Lord's work, planting a new church?

***

In July 1996, Dolores developed back pain and after weeks of physical therapy and no relief the doctors ordered a MRI, which showed a ruptured disc. After multiple surgeries and rehabilitation, we were still praying for total recovery. Preaching about faith is one thing, living by faith is quite another. Telling others to have faith is easy when they are sick; however, when it is personal, it's hard. It's awful to have friends like Job had who ask, "What's wrong with you? Why are you sick? Why don't you get well?"

It makes even pastors ask, "Why Lord, why?" How dare we tell people to have faith, it will turn out all right, or it will be easy. It may not turn out all right, and it isn't easy, it is never easy to see a loved one suffer.

It was a long road, but praise the Lord for carrying us through; six months later, Dolores was walking around the block and back to work. We praised the Lord and thanked Him for her healing. We thanked all those who cared about us and helped us during that time—financially, prayerfully, and emotionally.

***

What I have written is a far cry from the modern-day preaching of "pretend" Christianity, which proclaims that if you have faith, you will have wealth, health, and everything will turn out nice and easy for you.

Why didn't someone tell Jesus' disciples that? It could have spared them from being beaten, flogged, imprisoned, martyred, shipwrecked, hungry, and thirsty. And what about Christian martyrs David Livingstone, Nate Saint, Chet Bitterman, Jim Elliott, C.T. Studd, Hudson Taylor, and Paul Carlson; or the 35 missionaries who went to Ghana between the years of 1835–1870, only two of them lived more than two years.

In spite of all this "real" Christianity, the Gospel took root and grew.

Hebrews 11 tells us the reality of our faith:

> *All these people died still believing what God had promised them. They did not receive what was promised, but they saw it all from a distance and welcomed it. They agreed that they were foreigners and nomads here on earth.*
> *Women received their loved ones back again from death. But others were tortured, refusing to turn from God in order to be set free. They placed their hope in a better life after the resurrection. Some were jeered at, and their backs were cut open with whips. Others were chained in prisons. Some died by stoning, some were sawed in half, and others were killed with the sword. Some went about wearing skins of sheep and goats, destitute and oppressed and mistreated. They were too good for this world, wandering over deserts and mountains, hiding in caves and holes in the ground. All these people earned a good reputation because of their faith, yet none of them received all that God had promised. For God had something better in mind for us, so that they would not reach perfection without us* (Hebrews 11:35-40 NLT).

***

June 17, 2001. It is Father's Day and how wonderful it is to get cards, calls, and gifts from my sons. But my greatest reward in life is to have four sons who are honorable men, good husbands, and great fathers. Their greatest accomplishments are being God-fearing, God-honoring, and God-obeying men. Oh, how I wish I would have given more time and attention to being a father to them, giving them compliments and encouraging them more. I trust that my sons will do the right thing, no matter how poorly I have done as a father. I hope that all of their Father's Days are as blessed as mine have been.

***

While working in the real estate business, I have observed that self-employed people are much healthier than people who are employed by companies and the government. Self-employed people get up and work even if they don't feel good. Seldom do they call in sick or go on disability.

In 2004, I have worked as hard and as much as possible. I have transacted $170,000 of business so far this year; bought another apartment house, rented it, and put a new roof on the garage. Our financial situation seems to be stable for the first time in a long time. What a blessing!

Note
1. I highly recommend reading an excellent article about Chet Bitterman written by Melissa Paredes, "A Cause Worth Living For," October 31, 2016, Wycliffe Bible Translators; https://www.wycliffe.org/blog/featured/a-cause-worth-living-for; accessed September 9, 2021.

****

21
After the Earthquake

The Lord said, "Go out and stand on the mountain in the presence of the Lord, for the Lord is about to pass by." Then a great and powerful wind tore the mountains apart and shattered the rocks before the Lord, but the Lord was not in the wind. After the wind there was an earthquake, but the Lord was not in the earthquake. After the earthquake came a fire, but the Lord was not in the fire. And after the fire came a gentle whisper (1 Kings 19:11-12 NIV).

In January 2010, Haiti and the Dominican Republic experienced a large-scale, 7.0 magnitude earthquake with numerous aftershocks. *Britannica* reports of the damage:

> The collapsed buildings defining the landscape of the disaster area came as a consequence of Haiti's lack of building codes. Without adequate reinforcement, the buildings disintegrated under the force of the quake, killing or trapping their occupants. In Port-au-Prince the cathedral and the National Palace were both heavily damaged, as were the United Nations headquarters, national penitentiary, and parliament building. The city, already beset by a strained and inadequate infrastructure and still recovering from the two tropical storms and two hurricanes of August–September 2008, was ill-equipped to deal with such a disaster. Other affected areas of the country—faced with comparable weaknesses—were similarly unprepared.
>
> In the aftermath of the quake, efforts by citizens and international aid organizations to provide medical assistance, food, and water to survivors were hampered by the failure of the electric power system (which already was unreliable), loss of communication lines, and roads blocked with debris. A week after the event, little aid had reached beyond Port-au-Prince; after another week, supplies were being distributed only sporadically to other urban areas. Operations to rescue those trapped under the wreckage—which had freed over 100 people—had mostly ceased two weeks into the crisis, as hope that anyone could have survived for that length of time without food or water began to fade. However, there were still

occasional recoveries of people who had managed to survive such confinement for weeks by rationing the meagre supplies available to them.

It was estimated that some three million people were affected by the quake—nearly one-third of the country's total population. Of these, over one million were left homeless in the immediate aftermath. In the devastated urban areas, the displaced were forced to squat in ersatz cities composed of found materials and donated tents. Looting—restrained in the early days following the quake—became more prevalent in the absence of sufficient supplies and was exacerbated in the capital by the escape of several thousand prisoners from the damaged penitentiary. In the second week of the aftermath, many urbanites began streaming into outlying areas, either of their own volition or as a result of governmental relocation programs engineered to alleviate crowded and unsanitary conditions.

Because many hospitals had been rendered unusable, survivors were forced to wait days for treatment and, with morgues quickly reaching capacity, corpses were stacked in the streets. The onset of decay forced the interment of many bodies in mass graves, and recovery of those buried under the rubble was impeded by a shortage of heavy-lifting equipment, making death tolls difficult to determine. Figures released by Haitian government officials at the end of March placed the death toll at 222,570 people, though there was significant disagreement over the exact figure, and some estimated that nearly a hundred thousand more had perished. In January 2011, Haitian officials announced the revised figure of 316,000 deaths. The draft of a report commissioned by the U.S. government and made public in May 2011 drastically revised the estimate downward to no more than 85,000. Officials from the U.S. Agency for International Development (USAID) later acknowledged inconsistencies in data acquisition. Given the difficulty of observing documentation procedures in the rush to dispose of the dead, it was considered unlikely that a definitive total would ever be established.

> Further deaths occurred as serious injuries went untreated in the absence of medical staff and supplies. The orphans created by these mass mortalities—as well as those whose parents had died prior to the quake—were left vulnerable to abuse and human trafficking. Though adoptions of Haitian children by foreign nationals—particularly in the United States—were expedited, the process was slowed by the efforts of Haitian and foreign authorities to ensure that the children did not have living relatives, as orphanages had often temporarily accommodated the children of the destitute.[1]

Before the dust settled, Jeff and a group went to Miami but couldn't fly into Haiti, so they chartered a small plane and were there within a few days. After about a week, a number of us flew into the Dominican Republic and then went by car to Haiti. The airport in Haiti was still shut down. There is a very great difference between the infrastructure of Haiti and the Dominican Republic.

The devastation was unbelievable and there were mass gravesites along Route 1 leaving Port-au-Prince.

Some wonder if Haiti is cursed. The country has gone through so much torture and torment by evil governments and unscrupulous people over many years—as well as numerous natural disasters. In 2016 Hurricane Matthew hit Haiti, and in August 2021, Haiti experienced yet another devastating earthquake:

> Weeks after an earthquake killed more than 2,000 people in Haiti, the country is struggling to recover in the face of a public health crisis, a democracy rocked by a presidential assassination earlier this summer and longstanding social inequality. Jim Braude was joined on Greater Boston by Dr. Louise Ivers, a former resident of Haiti and the executive director of Massachusetts General Hospital's Center for Global Health, to discuss the challenges she saw on her recent return there to help with recovery efforts. Ivers described the conditions as "devastating" and said that gang activity has made recovery challenging for a region already struggling.

> "It's important to remember that this part of Haiti, this southern part, is already quite rural. Even on a good day, the roads are quite tricky. Access to water, food security is already a challenge," she said. "And just five years ago, Hurricane Matthew devastated this whole area.... People here are still recovering their livelihood from that."[2]

In 2010, we had just finished moving the children from the old orphanage in Port-au-Prince to the new orphanage at Willimson when the earthquake hit. If they would not have been moved, many would probably have suffered injury. The old orphanage was in the area where there was a lot of damage. We were thanking God for the timing of the move.

We had just finished the new orphanage complex, so the children were safe. The facilities were built better and it is some distance from the center of the earthquake. Some of the buildings where they were had been badly damaged. It would have been trauma for them had they still been there.

Unfortunately people who worked at the orphanage experienced death in the family or members of their family were missing. Consequently, many left instead of staying to take care of the children, so it was difficult for us to be fully staffed and organized.

We saw or met people daily who had lost a limb, was injured, and/or lost a family member. The Haitian overseer of the orphanage lived with her elderly mother right in the earthquake area. They slept out in the open at night because of the rumblings of additional aftershocks.

I didn't have very many friends who lived in Port-au-Prince, except Reverend Jules who lived in a cement house, that fortunately was not destroyed. But there was a tent city in the field beside his house. Nevertheless, they were holding school in a little tent only a few days later. But the people overall were desperate.

It always takes a long time cleaning up the rubble and debris. And then there is repairing of government buildings, hotels, the airport, etc. Some of the newer structures have been built better. But the slums are still the slums—never improved or rebuilt.

Billy Graham's son's organization, Samaritan's Purse, built a lot of small houses on vacant land, which was a blessing. So now there are people who have houses to replace the mostly ramshackle homes that were destroyed.

Haiti will always have a special place in my heart and I'm so pleased that our children and grandchildren have that special bond as well.

As Mother Teresa said, "If you can't feed a hundred people, then feed just one." And that is what we tried to do in Haiti—touch one person at a time with the Gospel of Jesus Christ.

Which reminds me of the starfish story, which you have probably heard or read but worth sharing here again:

> One day a man was walking along the beach when he noticed a boy picking up something and gently throwing it into the ocean. Approaching the boy, he asked, "What are you doing?" The youth replied, "Throwing starfish back into the ocean. The surf is up and the tide is going out. If I don't throw them back, they'll die." "Son," the man said, "don't you realize there are miles and miles of beach and hundreds of starfish? You can't make a difference!" After listening politely, the boy bent down, picked up another starfish, and threw it back into the surf. Then, smiling at the man, he said, "I made a difference for that one."[3]

Notes

1. Richard Pallardy, "2010 Haiti earthquake," *Britannica;* https://www.britannica.com/event/2010-Haiti-earthquake; accessed September 9, 2021.
2. Greater Boston Staff, "Three Weeks After Deadly Earthquake, Haiti Struggles to Recover," September 8, 2021, *CBH NEWS Local NPR,* https://www.wgbh.org/news/international-news/2021/09/08/three-weeks-after-deadly-earthquake-haiti-struggles-to-recover; accessed September 9, 2021.
3. Original starfish story written by Loren Eisley.

****

22

Living From the Heart

Today, in the year 2021, I live from the heart—my heart for God, family, the unsaved, and Haiti, always Haiti where I learned the most about myself and God's calling.

Writing over the years has been a joy and a chore—I have to use my brain to write and that's sometimes hard because it requires removing the clutter there, just like the clutter in kitchen drawers and on our desks. If our life is busy, it is because of clutter stuff, junk stuff; and if we complain we are too busy for Christ, family, or friends, it is because there is too much junk in our life. If all our closets are full and all our storage sheds are full, our lives are out of control.

The lighter we travel, the more we are at peace. I don't want to leave much behind when I go to Heaven, and I don't want much stuff to worry about while I wait for Heaven. Stuff is not worth much compared to family and friends. God promises to supply all our needs, so why do we need bigger storage barns and houses with more closets?

What stuff is cluttering my life, taking my time, robbing my joy, hindering my relationship with family and lessening my interest in heavenly matters? Taking inventory is wise.

***

As for Haiti today, the circumstances 20 years ago remain the same today in the island nation. The following is an article from *CBN News* dated September 9, 2021:

> In Haiti, suffering is still at a historic high following two natural disasters, a presidential assassination, and now, a delay in the start of the school year.
>
> The August 14th earthquake killed at least 2,248 Haitians and injured more than 12,000. It destroyed 53,000 homes and damaged tens of thousands.

Three days later, Tropical Storm Grace flooded the streets, adding to the misery of the country's 11 million citizens.

The humanitarian agency Operation Blessing reports that the government and UNICEF have assessed one-third of Haiti's 2,800 schools in the affected areas, finding at least two-thirds are damaged and 15% are destroyed....

The Haitian government has delayed the start of the school year but Emmanuela Delsoin, a spokeswoman for Operation Blessing, says Haitians aren't sure when classrooms will open as rebuilding right now is fraught with challenges. The earthquake struck the southwest part of the country, cutting off access to many areas and making it difficult to transport supplies and aid.

“So many schools have collapsed so the minister of education has had to postpone the re-entry, but everyone is wondering how,” said Delsoin.

In the southern port city of Les Cayes, Samaritan's Purse flew in an emergency field hospital.

“We brought in a lot of medical relief supplies, the infrastructure we need to operate in this kind of environment where there is little electricity,” said Monte Oitker, a medical engineering technician with Samaritan’s Purse. “So we came fully prepared and self-contained.”

While aid from a multitude of NGOs is welcome, it’s not nearly enough.

Operation Blessing reports that health facilities are overwhelmed. Plus, more than 100,000 people need clean drinking water, and there’s growing concern about the risk of diseases such as cholera and malaria.

Thousands of families still have no place to sleep after their homes were destroyed.

And following the July assassination of President Jovenel Moise, gang control and violence are on the rise.

It's chasing away potential foreign investors, slowing down relief, and destabilizing the country at the very moment it needs to come together.[1]

***

These days, as in most days in the age of infinite news and social media sites, matters of the heart are mostly on the back burner. Politics, on the other hand, clutter the airwaves, the Internet, and conversations far and wide. It is the stuff of controversy on both sides of the aisle. Why do we pray for God to intercede in presidential, state, and local elections? He's not voting, we are. Is it God's fault who we elect?

Are we to obey the government or God? I believe we must obey God who speaks to our hearts, rather than government.

Jesus' conversation with the leaders who "sent spies pretending to be honest men" is enlightening:

They tried to get Jesus to say something that could be reported to the Roman governor so he would arrest Jesus. "Teacher," they said, "we know that you speak and teach what is right and are not influenced by what others think. You teach the way of God truthfully. Now tell us—is it right for us to pay taxes to Caesar or not?"

He saw through their trickery and said, "Show me a Roman coin. Whose picture and title are stamped on it?"

"Caesar's," they replied.

"Well then," he said, "give to Caesar what belongs to Caesar, and give to God what belongs to God."

So they failed to trap him by what he said in front of the people. Instead, they were amazed by his answer, and they became silent (Luke 20:20-26 NLT).

And Paul tells Timothy:

> *I urge, then, first of all, that petitions, prayers, intercession and thanksgiving be made for all people—for kings and all those in authority, that we may live peaceful and quiet lives in all godliness and holiness* (1 Timothy 2:1-2 NIV).

When living from the heart, our interaction with authority—government, local, church, state, workplace, national—must be based on seeking the Kingdom of God first, always.

Doing right is sometimes costly, but may I say it is always worth it. Many in the church don't want to be questioned or confronted, especially about money or teachings. Yet there must be accountability.

Likewise on a national level, how can God allow a pro-death candidate to be elected to the highest position of authority in the country? Is God more powerful than our vote? I believe in the sovereignty of God and the responsibility of humans. The sovereignty of God makes us responsible for our choices. Please tell me, can a person be a Christian and vote for someone who believes babies should be murdered for the sake of convenience? "Choice" makes my gut churn. We must live from the heart and speak for the unborn who have the right to life.

***

Celebrating the Christ child's birth with our boys and their families at Christmastime brings all hearts together as one. Dolores and I thank God for blessing us with four wonderful sons and four special daughters-in-law, and our dear grandchildren. Everything this world has to offer pales in significance to our family. I pray for all the young ones, that they will grow up with clear godly values.

Lord, help us to thank You and see things from Your point of view. We pray that every president and governmental authority will rely on You—not lean on their own understanding.

***

I am so very proud of our family mission that was founded in 2012 by our eldest son, Jeff, and his wife, Terri. The following is from the **CrossRoads Mission HAITI** website:

> CrossRoads Mission HAITI is an independent, non-denominational ministry designed to support and uplift the people of Haiti. "I never saw darkness that dark" Jeff remembers as a six-year-old boy living in Haiti with his missionary parents, lying in bed, waiting for sleep while listening to the sound of distant voodoo drums.
>
> "There is something about Haiti that has me" became the new drumbeat which drove Jeff to seek opportunities to participate on projects in Haiti. After volunteering for more than four years as part-time missionaries, both Terri and Jeff felt God's call, leading them in a new direction, taking a road to further assist Haitian people in need.
>
> CrossRoads is not about one specific project, but seeks opportunities to connect with communities and villages where they can share Christ's love with a people the Swopes and their family and friends have come to love deeply.
>
> CrossRoads Mission HAITI is a faith-based program that currently, offers education to the children of families who are unable to pay for Haitian schooling, and supports community Bible school programs. "We are about sharing Jesus' love to other
>
> **Our Mission**
>
> CrossRoads was founded with a specific purpose given to us by God. We continue to stand at the crossroads an listen for God's voice, his prompting to step out in faith where He would lead us (Jeremiah 6:16). Obedience to the one true God is the cornerstone of our foundation with integrity and sincerity; the key qualities we believe are essential to bring praise and honor to God in everything we do. We want to grow in response to the needs that God identifies for us and not to glorify ourselves.

God, our board and our benefactors must hold us accountable to these beliefs and values.

The Boucan Church

The Boucan Church came under our leadership in 2018 and is located 2-1/2 hours from the main road up in the mountains. The congregation had been meeting in a stick structure with tarps with 25 people in attendance. In February 2019, a new church building was built. Many men from the community helped with this project, alongside of a team of six men from the states, including an electrician, who wired the church for electricity so they could hold services at night. Since February 2019, the congregation has grown to 125.

Our Family

Jeff and Terri Swope, Founders, CrossRoads Mission HAITI. Jeff is also the owner of JL Swope Construction. Their son, Conlan, is a project manager for a construction management company, and his wife, Melissa, is a physical therapist. Daughter Kelsey is a mother of three.[2]

***

In 2008, Jeff built three orphanage buildings, two school buildings, a large church building, and a rehab building where crippled children received physical rehabilitation. He installed all the generators needed, the wells for water, the solar systems, and so forth.

These building were finished just before the earthquake shook the island in 2010. The buildings were strong and stood firm.

From that project he built churches and schools, as well as conducted a medical clinic every year. The medical clinic participants were divided into several locations—some were in the extreme mountain areas where we had to travel difficult and dangerous terrain over poor roads, having to use a four-wheel drive pick-up and all-terrain vehicles.

There are people who live all over the mountains in Haiti. They survive off of the land, farming the steepest of the mountains. It's really amazing their skills and resolve to survive on their own determination. Staple crops are mainly sorghum, beans, and corn. They also grow mango and avocado trees. If there is a ravine with water, banana trees will flourish.

***

Contrasting the idyllic beauty of the mountains was the "food riots" in Port-au-Prince in the early to mid-2000s.

The first traumatic experience we had was when Jeff and I started taking teams to Haiti as part of his organization Crossroads Mission Haiti. People were rioting because of the lack of food and the excessively high prices of common food. During the riots, all the roads were blocked, preventing people from going to or coming from the airport.

Several times there were riots that interfered with our being able to get to the airport.

Jeff knew that the looters and rioters were not early risers so he told us, "We'll leave at 5 o'clock tomorrow morning to go to the airport. That way you'll be there when it's time for your flight." That meant possibly sitting at the airport the whole day if the flight didn't leave until in the evening. That was how we got out during the food riots.[3]

***

Living from the heart has been my goal over the waning years of my life. Being obedient to God and supportive of my family are my priorities. Some "one-liners" that have defined my life include the following:

- We are not saved because we work; we work because we are saved.
- Works are not evidence of salvation; obedience is evidence of salvation.
- There is no great work ever done before we bear the cross; take up our cross and follow Jesus.
- There is never a great accomplishment without a great sacrifice.

- God has never used anyone in doing a great work for Him, until after that person has crucified everything in life—security, success, future, home, family, houses, land, job, reputation, fame, power, prestige, ability, intellect and academic, and YES willing to risk their life to obey the will and call of God.

Notes

1. Heather Sells, "53,000 Homes Destroyed, Schools Wiped Out: Why Is It so Hard to Get Aid to Haiti at This Point of Dire Need?"; *CBN News,* September 9, 2021; https://www1.cbn.com/cbnnews/world/2021/september/53-000-homes-destroyed-schools-wiped-out-why-is-it-so-hard-to-get-aid-to-haiti-at-this-point-of-dire-need; accessed September 10, 2021.

2. CrossRoads Mission Haiti website: https://crossroadshaiti.org/; accessed September 10, 2021.

3. An insightful article about this time in Haiti's history was written by Mark Schuller on April 29, 2008, "Haitian Food Riots Unnerving but Not Surprising"; *Worldpress.org;* https://www.worldpress.org/Americas/3131.cfm#:~:text=The%20food%20riots%20in%20Haiti%20were%20also%20a,long-term%20underdevelopment%20and%20inequalities%20in%20the%20world%20system; accessed September 10, 2021.

****

Epilogue

In a nutshell…

I am now 82 years old and am involved with a Celebrate Recovery program. Dolores and I live in Quarryville, Pennsylvania.

Our eldest son, Jeff, bought our farm that was my dad's farm in 2016. He operates J.L. Swope Construction. Our son Kirby bought Grandpap's farm in Maddensville. He works for a construction company. Our son Kevin is an owner of DICE Office Equipment. Our youngest son Jamie works for a construction company.

Still left to be done, my wish list:

- I wish I could lead one more person to Christ.
- I wish I could make one more trip to Haiti.
- I wish I could plant one more church.

The good Lord has never left me down and I know He is still in control of my life. Whatever He has in store for me before taking me to Heaven, I welcome with open arms and a softened heart.

***

If you are wise and understand God's ways, prove it by living an honorable life, doing good works with the humility that comes from wisdom (James 3:13 NLT).

Made in the USA
Middletown, DE
06 March 2023